# Pâtisserie OF ITALY

### JENI WRIGHT

## McGRAW-HILL BOOK COMPANY

New York   St. Louis   San Francisco
Hamburg   Mexico

The author would like to thank Elisa Surini for her invaluable help and advice and Mary Pope for her assistance with testing the recipes.

*All eggs are large unless otherwise stated*

First U.S. publication by McGraw-Hill Book Company in 1988

Text copyright © Macdonald & Co (Publishers) Ltd and
Jeni Wright 1988
Photographs © Macdonald & Co (Publishers) Ltd 1988

First published in Great Britain in 1988
by Macdonald & Co (Publishers) Ltd
London & Sydney

A member of BPCC plc

1 2 3 4 5 6 7 8     8 9 2 1 0 9 8

Library of Congress Cataloging-in-Publication Data

Wright, Jeni.
Pâtisserie of Italy.
"A Macdonald Orbis book"–Verso t.p.
1. Pastry–Italy  2. Cookery, Italian.
I. Title
TX773.W798  1988  641.8'65  87-35387
ISBN 0-07-072090-8


Typeset by Tradespools, Frome

Printed and bound in Great Britain by
Purnell Book Production Limited
A member of BPCC plc


Editor: Gillian Prince
Text Editor: Norma MacMillan
Art Director: Bobbie Colegate-Stone
Designer: Frances de Rees
Photographer: Grant Symon
Stylist: Sue Russell
Home Economist: Janice Murfitt

# Contents

# *Introduction*

Until unification in 1861, Italy was divided into separate regions each with its own government, customs – and culinary heritage. "Italian cooking" as such did not exist, and despite unification, it still doesn't today. Clearly there are common links between one region and another, but in every modern Italian cook's repertoire there remain distinct regional differences in the way dishes are prepared and a fierce local identity and pride. Even within the same locality no two bakers will bake the same cake alike: from the simple rustic breads of the countryside to the elaborate concoctions of the professional *pasticciere,* the main features are individuality and freedom of expression.

Breadmaking was introduced to the Romans by the Greeks in the second century before Christ, but it was the Arabs 1000 years later who brought sweets, cakes and desserts to Sicily and the southern regions of Italy. Honey was the universal sweetener in those days – it was not until the Middle Ages that sugar came to Italy by way of the Venetian traders, and then it was a luxury restricted to the very rich. Nonetheless, the Italians rapidly acquired a sweet tooth, particularly those in the south.

In Renaissance days when interest in gastronomy was at its height, Italian pastry cooks quickly made a name for themselves creating lavish desserts and confections for grand banquets and state occasions. The Medici of Florence were considered the culinary masters, and by the sixteenth century the reputation of Florentine chefs had spread to France when Catherine de' Medici took her own chefs with her for her marriage to the dauphin, later to become Henri II. French pâtissiers are thus indebted to the Italians, and it is a fact that while English noblemen of the 1800s employed chefs from France, they invariably chose Italian pastry chefs rather than French.

There is then a long tradition of baking throughout Italy and undoubtedly Italians have a sweet tooth, yet for everyday family meals it is quite rare for a dessert to be served. Most Italian meals finish with cheese and fresh fruit, or at the most an ice cream or a sherbet. *Dolci* are held in such high esteem that they are almost always enjoyed on their own, not at the end of a meal when stomachs are full and appetites sated. They are eaten with a glass of wine or liqueur and a cup of coffee – as a special treat at any time of day, often at a café rather than at home, or even for a late evening snack. Every town boasts at least one *pasticceria* and it is usual for the Italian housewife to buy special breads, cakes, pastries and cookies to serve at home, particularly for occasions like birthdays and festivals such as Christmas and Easter. There are countless different regional specialties for these occasions. This is not to say that *dolci* are difficult to make at home, but simply that it is traditional for them to be bought from local high-class specialists – a custom that has developed in many other European countries.

Recipes are rarely used by bakers and pastry chefs; they tend to rely more on their sense of touch, taste, sight and smell rather than the written word. Bakers take great pleasure in *fantasia* – the art of experimentation – which means that every pastry may be slightly different each time it is made. Originality and individuality are the keynotes in Italian pâtisserie, and while the recipes in this book may be followed to the letter, it is more likely that an Italian cook would interpret them loosely. Different flavorings may be used for example, cakes may be baked in more unusual shapes, tarts topped with different fruits. The beauty of Italian pastry-making is that one is allowed total freedom of expression.

## INGREDIENTS

Italian cooks are always particular over their choice of ingredients. Quality and freshness are of utmost importance and generally speaking no expense is spared to get the right ingredient. There are very few special or unusual items required for any of the recipes in this book, but the following list will be useful when shopping for specific ingredients.

*Candied fruits and candied peel:* Both of these are used extensively in Italian pâtisserie especially in recipes from Sicily and the south. Use the kind found in specialty stores and health food shops which are sweet, succulent and full of natural flavor, the nearest equivalent to the beautiful candied fruits for which the Sicilians are so famous. Do not use the chopped candied peel that is available in plastic tubs from supermarkets as this will give a synthetic flavor and chewy texture. Candied peel bought loose from a health food shop can sometimes be quite hard (particularly if it is citron peel). Soak it in warm water for about 20 minutes to make it easier to cut or chop.

*Chocolate:* For recipes with chocolate, use a top quality semisweet or bittersweet chocolate. This is made from unsweetened baking chocolate (the pure form of the chocolate liquor) with sugar and extra cocoa butter added. Semisweet chocolate is available in packages containing individually-wrapped 1 ounce squares. Do not substitute unsweetened chocolate in these recipes.

*Extracts:* Professional Italian bakers use very powerful, highly concentrated extracts such as *aroma di limone* (lemon) and *aroma di arancia* (orange), and there are even special mixtures to flavor whole cakes such as *aroma di panettone*. Vanilla and almond extracts are used in many breads, cakes and cookies; when buying these, be sure to check the label and buy only pure, natural extracts or oils – these are available from most supermarkets. Bottles labeled "imitation" or "flavoring" are synthetic and should not be used.

*Polenta flour:* This is a very finely ground cornmeal used in breads and cakes. Ordinary yellow cornmeal, sold in every supermarket, can be used in all recipes. However, if you buy it as polenta flour from an Italian specialty store, be sure to buy finely ground polenta for baking purposes, not the coarse polenta which is cooked to be served as an accompaniment to savory dishes.

*Savoiardi:* Italian ladyfinger cookies, called *savoiardi,* are used in many refrigerated cakes. Crisp, sweet and light, they are better quality than the type found in packages in supermarkets. Look for *savoiardi* in Italian gourmet shops; although more expensive than ordinary ladyfingers, they lend a more authentic flavor and texture to Italian desserts.

*Coarse sugar:* Italian bakers are fond of sprinkling coarse sugar on top of countless cakes, breads and buns – they are traditional on the Milanese Easter cake *Colomba,* for example. They do give an attractive professional finish, but unfortunately they are only available commercially. Coarsely crushed sugar cubes or broken rock candy give a similar effect.

*Vanilla sugar:* Vanilla is a popular flavoring in Italian pâtisserie, and vanilla sugar is used extensively. Purchased vanilla sugar can be used, but a fresher flavor can be obtained by making vanilla sugar at home. Simply bury a vanilla bean in an airtight jar of sugar; it will flavor the sugar after about 2 weeks and will then keep indefinitely.

### Liqueurs and Fortified Wine

Alcohol is frequently added to cake and refrigerated cake mixtures, sugar syrups, fruit toppings and creamy fillings. Apart from the usual brandy, grappa and rum, there are a number of specific Italian drinks that appear again and again. They are easy to find at good liquor stores, and as they can be used as after-dinner liqueurs as well as for cooking, are well worth buying to achieve an authentic flavor.

*Amaretto* is a liqueur made from bitter apricot kernels. It comes from Saronno, which gives its name to the famous macaroons from the same town, *amaretti di Saronno.* In baking, Amaretto is used to heighten flavor when almonds are used; it has more of a "kick" than almond extract.

*Aurum* is an unusual orange liqueur from Pescara. It has quite a sharp tang and makes the most delicious after-dinner liqueur. If difficult to obtain, there are many other orange-flavoured liqueurs which may be used instead.

*Kahlúa* is a coffee liqueur from Mexico which is used in some Italian desserts, most notably Tirami Su (page 48). *Tia Maria,* which is also widely available, is very similar and can be used instead.

*Maraschino* is a liqueur made from marasca cherries which comes in a most unusual tall bottle covered in straw. It has a distinctive aroma and flavor, but any cherry brandy can be used instead.

*Marsala* is a fortified wine from Sicily which has a flavor reminiscent of burnt sugar. It is an essential ingredient in many Sicilian specialties and there is no substitute for its unique flavor. Both dry and sweet Marsala are available, but it is the sweet Marsala which is used in baking. Do not use Marsala *all'uovo,* which contains eggs.

*Sambuca* is an Italian anis liqueur with a dry, licorice flavor. Any French *pastis* can be substituted if easier to obtain.

*Strega* is a beautiful, golden-yellow liqueur made from over 70 herbs. Rich and sweet, it is used in many desserts. There is no equivalent.

### Cheese

*Mascarpone:* This fresh cheese is sold in plastic tubs at most good Italian specialty stores. It is very rich (containing 90 percent fat) with a velvety consistency. Italians eat it with fresh fruit and sugar as the French do *fromage frais* and use it in many desserts, particularly refrigerated cakes. It is quite bland in flavor; thick fresh cream may be used as a substitute.

*Ricotta:* Ricotta is a soft, fresh white cheese. Originally it was made from goat's milk, but nowadays it is usually made from either ewe's or cow's milk, or from a mixture of these. It has a fat content of 15–20 percent, depending on the type of milk it is made from, and can be bought loose from Italian specialty cheese shops – it comes in an attractive molded cake shape. Fresh ricotta has poor keeping qualities and should be bought and used on the same day otherwise it becomes very acid. If you are unable to obtain it, use the ricotta sold in supermarkets or sieved cottage cheese instead.

### HINTS ON BAKING WITH YEAST

The recipes in this book are straightforward and easy to follow. No particular skills are required apart from patience and a steady hand when it comes to decorating and piping. For the yeast chapter, however, it is necessary to follow certain basic rules to achieve success every time. Yeast has a reputation as a temperamental ingredient, and it is wise to know how to deal with it!

Fresh compressed yeast is used throughout the recipes in this book, but this does not mean that active dry yeast cannot be used if you find it more convenient. Active dry yeast is more concentrated than fresh – as a general rule, ½ ounce active dry yeast is equivalent to 1 ounce fresh, but always check the instructions on the package before use as these may vary. Also check the method of incorporating the yeast as some varieties are mixed with the dry ingredients, some with liquid. When buying fresh yeast, check that it is really fresh or it will not work. Buy it from a busy local bakery and check that it is creamy in color and cool to the touch. When broken, it should crumble.

Before starting any recipe containing yeast it is important to get the right warm atmosphere in the kitchen. Warm bowls, utensils and hands in hot water, and warm the flour through in a low oven. In all of the recipes in this book, the yeast is first made into a batter with some of the liquid and flour; this is the best method to use for the enriched doughs containing fat, sugar and egg which are so common in Italian baking. These ingredients retard the growth of the yeast and therefore rising is much slower than with plain doughs. Salt is not added to the flour for the batter at this stage as this could retard the action of the yeast or even kill it altogether. Liquid should be at blood heat (100–110°F) for it to activate the yeast quickly. Liquid that is below blood heat will still activate the yeast but it will take longer. Hotter liquid will kill the yeast, so take care not to heat it above 140°F. When mixing the ingredients together, add the specified quantity of liquid all at once and mix it in quickly. Sometimes a little more liquid may be required, depending on the absorbency of the flour and the exact size of the eggs, etc. – if you are experienced at handling dough you will know the exact feel of it.

The recipes in this book give instructions for mixing the ingredients and kneading the dough with a dough hook in a heavy duty (countertop) electric mixer. This takes all the hard work out of breadmaking as the gluten is quickly developed and the dough becomes smooth and elastic in as short a time as 2–3 minutes. If you do not have a countertop mixer, mix the ingredients in a bowl with a wooden spoon, then knead by hand on the work surface. With enriched Italian doughs this can be quite hard – you will probably have to knead for at least 10–15 minutes.

From the initial addition of the liquid through the mixing, kneading and rising, remember that the temperature should not rise above 140°F or the yeast will be killed and the dough will not rise. For rising in summer the dough can generally be left out in the kitchen as long as it is in a draft-free place. In winter, a warm linen cupboard or an unheated oven with a pan of very hot water placed in the bottom are two favorite spots for rising dough.

*Delicious Cake*

# Sweet Raised Breads

## Milanese Christmas Fruit Bread

### — PANETTONE DI MILANO —

*The distinctively shaped boxes of Panettone can be seen hanging from the ceilings of Italian food shops all over the world at Christmastime, because Panettone has truly become the traditional Italian Christmas cake. Light and airy, filled with candied fruit and raisins and flavored with vanilla, it is a great favorite with the Italians at breakfast, not only at Christmas but also during the rest of the year. Panettone is said to have been invented in the 15th century by a Milanese baker called Toni. Originally called pan de Toni after him, over the centuries it has become known simply as Panettone.*

*Very few Italians make Panettone at home, simply because the commercial varieties are so good. This version is not quite so open-textured as the kind that you buy, but the technique of double rising makes it very similar and equally as good. The characteristic tall shape of Panettone cannot be made without a proper Panettone mold, and unfortunately these are unavailable outside Italy. However, using a cake pan and a foil collar gives a very similar result and the tying of the "waist" of the bread with ribbon before serving is extremely effective. If you prefer a straight-sided bread without a "waist," then line the inside of the pan with foil, although this is more tricky than tying the foil outside as given here. Another alternative is to use an empty 6 inch diameter catering-size ice cream or preserve mold which is 7–9 inches tall. Grease it well, then line the bottom with nonstick parchment paper and dust with flour before use.*

**MAKES 1 LOAF WEIGHING ABOUT 2 lb**

| |
|---|
| 2¾ cups bread flour |
| 1 oz compressed yeast |
| ⅔ cup milk, at blood heat |
| 1 egg |
| 2 egg yolks |
| 3 tbsp vanilla sugar |
| 1 tsp salt |
| 1 stick butter, melted |
| ½ cup finely chopped candied fruit |
| ½ cup golden raisins |
| finely grated zest of 1 orange |
| a pat of butter, to finish |

Sift the flour into the warmed bowl of a heavy duty (countertop) electric mixer. Cream the yeast in a separate warmed bowl with 2 tbsp of the milk, then work in 2 tbsp of the flour to make a batter. Cover with oiled plastic wrap and leave in a warm place until spongy – about 30 minutes.

Beat the egg and egg yolks together in a bowl, then stir in the vanilla sugar and salt. Mix the melted butter into the yeast mixture, then mix in the egg mixture.

Make a well in the center of the flour, add the yeast mixture and the remaining milk and work with the dough hook until the dough is smooth and elastic. Turn out on to a lightly floured surface and form into a ball. Clean and grease the bowl, then return the dough to it. Cover the bowl with oiled plastic wrap and leave in a warm place until the dough has doubled in bulk, about 1–2 hours.

Turn the dough out on to a lightly floured surface, punch down and knead until smooth and elastic again. Return to the bowl, cover again and leave to rise as before until doubled in bulk.

Meanwhile, grease a 3 inch deep, 6 inch round cake pan. Line the bottom with a circle of nonstick parchment paper, then grease the paper. Dust with flour, shaking off the excess. Tie a foil collar around the outside of the pan with string, to come 3 inches above the rim of the pan.

Turn the dough out and punch down again. Mix the candied fruit, raisins and orange zest together, add to the dough in 2 batches and knead in until evenly incorporated. Form into a 6 inch ball.

Put the ball of dough in the prepared pan, then cut a 3½ inch cross in the top with kitchen scissors. Cover with oiled plastic wrap and leave to rise again in a very warm place until the domed part of the dough has risen up to the top of the foil – 30 minutes to 1 hour. Meanwhile, preheat the oven to 400°F.

Uncover the pan, cut the cross again with scissors, then gently place the pat of butter in the center of the cross. Bake for 10 minutes, then lower the temperature to 350°F and bake for a further 40–45 minutes or until a skewer inserted into the center comes out clean.

Leave the Panettone to cool in the pan for a few minutes, then remove the foil collar. Gently place the pan on its side and carefully ease out the bread. Turn it the right way up and leave to cool on a wire rack. Tie ribbon around the "waist" of the bread before serving, if liked.

*Illustrated on page 14*

*Milanese Christmas Fruit Bread*

# *Almond Ring Cake*

## ———— CIAMBELLA MANDORLATA ————

*T*he word ciambella means "ring cake," and in Italy there are many different kinds, depending on
the region in which they are made. This version from Como is plain and simple, delicately
flavored with almonds. The Ciambella from Bologna on the other hand is rich and fruity, the one
from Abruzzo-Molisse is made with red wine and olive oil, and the one from Puglia with boiled and
mashed potatoes! Serve this Ciambella Mandorlata cut into thin slices, with jam or preserves. Or
split the cake through the middle and sandwich it together with jam. It is the perfect plain cake to
serve with tiny cups of strong, black espresso coffee.

**SERVES 8–10**

| | |
|---|---|
| 3¼ cups all-purpose flour | *Almond topping* |
| 4 tsp baking powder | a little beaten egg |
| pinch of salt | ½ cup sliced almonds |
| 4½ tbsp butter, softened | 3 tbsp coarse sugar or |
| ½ cup sugar | broken-up rock candy |
| 2 eggs, beaten | |
| almond extract | |
| 1 cup + 2 tbsp milk | |

Preheat the oven to 350°F. Grease a 5 cup ring mold and dust lightly with flour, shaking out any excess.

Sift the flour, baking powder and salt into a bowl. Set aside. Put the butter and sugar in a separate bowl
and beat until well blended. Add the beaten eggs a little at a time, beating well after each addition. Add a
few drops of almond extract and beat again until well mixed. Fold in the flour and milk a little at a time until
both are evenly incorporated to make a stiff dropping consistency.

Spoon into the prepared mold, level the surface and brush with beaten egg. Mix the almonds and sugar
together and sprinkle over the top. Bake for 45–50 minutes or until well risen and golden – a skewer inserted
into the cake should come out clean. Leave to rest in the mold for a few minutes, then invert a plate over the
mold and carefully unmold the cake on to it. Turn the cake the right way up on to a wire rack and leave to
cool completely. Before serving, cut into thin slices.

# *Rum-Flavored Milk Buns*

## —— CREMONESE ——

*As their name suggests, Cremonese come from Cremona in Lombardy, famous for its unusual mostarda di frutta or fruit relish, which is eaten with locally smoked and spiced meats. The region is renowned for its excellent dairy farming, and milk breads and buns are therefore common. Cremonese are unusual in that they are quite strongly flavored with rum.*

### MAKES 12

| | To finish |
|---|---|
| 3¾ cups bread flour | *To finish* |
| 1 oz compressed yeast | 1 egg, beaten |
| ⅔ cup water, at blood heat | 2½ tbsp coarse sugar or |
| ½ cup instant dry milk | broken-up rock candy |
| 2 tbsp butter | |
| ⅓ cup sugar | |
| pinch of salt | |
| ⅓ cup dark rum, at blood heat | |
| 1 egg, beaten | |

Sift the flour into the warmed bowl of a heavy duty (countertop) electric mixer. Cream the yeast in a separate warmed bowl with 2 tbsp of the water, then work in 2 tbsp of the flour to make a batter. Cover with oiled plastic wrap and leave in a warm place until spongy – about 30 minutes.

Meanwhile, dissolve the milk powder in the remaining water. Work the butter, sugar and salt into the flour. Make a well in the center, add the milk liquid, the yeast mixture, rum and egg and work with the dough hook until the dough is smooth and elastic. Turn out on to a well floured surface and form into a ball. Clean and grease the bowl, then return the dough to it. Cover the bowl with oiled plastic wrap and leave in a warm place until the dough has doubled in bulk, about 1–2 hours.

Turn the dough out on to a floured surface, punch down, then cut into 12 equal pieces. Form into balls and place them well apart on greased baking sheets. Cover with oiled plastic wrap and leave to rise again in a warm place until doubled in size – about 30 minutes. Meanwhile, preheat the oven to 375°F.

Uncover the buns, brush with the beaten egg and sprinkle with the sugar. Bake for 15–20 minutes or until golden. Transfer to a wire rack and leave to cool before serving.

*Illustrated on page 19*

# $\mathcal{S}$weet Little Yeast Buns

## BOCCONCINI DEL NONNO

*L*iterally translated, bocconcini del nonno means "grandfather's mouthfuls." Traditionally, these bite-sized buns are a great favorite with grandfathers, but this is probably due to the fact that they are quite heavily laced with Marsala more than anything else!*

**MAKES 32**

| |
|---|
| 3¾ cups bread flour |
| 1 oz compressed yeast |
| ¾ cup milk, at blood heat |
| 2 tbsp butter |
| 6 tbsp sugar |
| pinch of salt |
| 1 egg, beaten |
| 3 tbsp lemon juice |
| 2 tbsp Marsala wine, at blood heat |
| a little confectioners' sugar, to finish |

Sift the flour into the warmed bowl of a heavy duty (countertop) electric mixer. Cream the yeast in a separate warmed bowl with 2 tbsp of the milk, then work in 2 tbsp of the flour to make a batter. Cover with oiled plastic wrap and leave in a warm place until spongy – about 30 minutes.

Meanwhile, work the butter, sugar and salt into the flour. Make a well in the center, add the remaining milk, the yeast mixture, egg, lemon juice and Marsala and work with the dough hook until the dough is smooth and elastic. Turn out on to a well floured surface and form into a ball. Clean and grease the bowl, then return the dough to it. Cover the bowl with oiled plastic wrap and leave in a warm place until the dough has doubled in bulk, about 1–2 hours.

Turn the dough out on to a floured surface and punch down. Cut the dough in half, then into quarters. Cut each quarter in half, then each piece into 4, to make 32 equal pieces. Form the pieces into tiny bite-sized balls and place them well apart on greased baking sheets. Cover with oiled plastic wrap and leave to rise again in a warm place until doubled in size – about 30 minutes. Meanwhile, place a roasting pan filled with hot water on the floor of the oven, and preheat the oven to 425°F.

Uncover the buns and bake for 8–10 minutes or until golden brown. Transfer to a wire rack, sift confectioners' sugar lightly over the top and leave to cool before serving.

*Illustrated on page 18*

*Raisin and Walnut Bread & Sweet Little Yeast Buns*

*Rum-Flavored Milk Buns & Sweet Cornmeal Buns*

# *Raisin and Walnut Bread*

## ——— PANE DI UVA CON NOCI ———

*At first sight, this crusty bread appears to be made with whole wheat flour, as it has a nutty brown color and texture when sliced. In fact, it is made with white flour – it is the chopped walnuts which give the crumb of the bread a "whole wheat" appearance.*
*The quantities in this recipe are enough to make 2 loaves. Eat one fresh and freeze the other if you like – it will freeze beautifully for up to 1 week (after this time the crust may lift off). Any leftover stale bread is excellent served toasted and buttered for breakfast.*

**MAKES 2 LOAVES, EACH WEIGHING ABOUT 1¼ lb**

| |
|---|
| 4½ cups bread flour |
| ½ oz compressed yeast |
| 1⅔ cups water, at blood heat |
| 1 tbsp butter |
| 1 tbsp sugar |
| ½ tsp salt |
| 1¼ cups roughly chopped walnuts |
| 2 cups golden raisins |

Sift the flour into the warmed bowl of a heavy duty (countertop) electric mixer. Cream the yeast in a separate warmed bowl with 2 tbsp of the water, then work in 2 tbsp of the flour to make a batter. Cover with oiled plastic wrap and leave in a warm place until spongy – about 30 minutes

Meanwhile, work the butter, sugar and salt into the flour. Make a well in the center, add the remaining water and the yeast mixture and work with the dough hook until the dough is smooth and elastic. Turn out on to a lightly floured surface and form into a ball. Clean and grease the bowl, then return the dough to it. Cover the bowl with a sheet of oiled plastic wrap and leave in a warm place until the dough has doubled in bulk, about 1–2 hours.

Turn the dough out on to a lightly floured surface, punch down, then work in the walnuts and raisins. Form the dough into two 9 inch rolls, place on greased baking sheets and cover with oiled plastic wrap. Leave to rise again in a warm place until doubled in size – about 45 minutes to 1 hour. Meanwhile, preheat the oven to 425°F.

Uncover the loaves and bake for 10 minutes, then reduce the temperature to 375°F and bake for a further 25–30 minutes or until golden brown. Cover the loaves with parchment paper or foil during baking if they are browning too quickly. Transfer to a wire rack and leave to cool before serving.

*Illustrated on page 18*

# $\mathscr{S}$weet Cornmeal Buns

## — PAN MEINI —

*These buns, which come from Milan, were originally made to celebrate San Giorgio's Day on April 24. San Giorgio is the patron saint of dairy men, and the workers on dairy farms in Lombardy would mark the occasion by eating Pan Meini with cream. The buns are made a creamy yellow color from the inclusion of yellow cornmeal.*

### MAKES 16–18

| | |
|---|---|
| 2 cups bread flour | *Glaze* |
| 1 oz compressed yeast | 2 tbsp sugar |
| scant 1 cup water, at blood heat | 1 tbsp water |
| 1½ cups yellow cornmeal | 2 tbsp Sambuca liqueur (optional) |
| ½ cup sugar | |
| pinch of salt | |
| 1 stick butter, melted | |
| 2 egg yolks | |
| vanilla extract | |

Sift the flour into a warmed bowl. Put the yeast in the warmed bowl of a heavy duty (countertop) electric mixer and gradually blend in ⅔ cup of the water, then 1 cup of the sifted flour. Cover with oiled plastic wrap and leave to rise in a warm place for 20–45 minutes.

Sift the cornmeal, sugar and salt into the bowl of flour and mix together. Uncover the yeast bowl and add the melted butter, together with the remaining water, the cornmeal and flour mixture, the egg yolks and a few drops of vanilla extract. Work with the dough hook until the dough is smooth and elastic (it will be quite soft and sticky). Turn out on to a well floured surface and form into a ball. Clean and grease the bowl, then return the dough to it. Cover the bowl with oiled plastic wrap and leave in a warm place until the dough has doubled in bulk, about 1–2 hours.

Turn the dough out on to a floured surface, punch down, then divide into 16–18 portions. Shape into small balls and place them well apart on greased baking sheets. Cover with oiled plastic wrap and leave to rise again in a warm place until doubled in size – about 30 minutes. Meanwhile, preheat the oven to 425°F.

Uncover the buns and bake for 15–20 minutes or until they are golden brown and sound hollow when tapped on the base. Mix together the sugar and water for the glaze, brush on top of the buns and return to the oven for 1 minute until dry. Remove from the oven and brush with the liqueur, if using. Transfer to a wire rack and leave to cool before serving.

*Illustrated on page 19*

# Chocolate Bread

## —————————— PANE AL CIOCCOLATO ——————————

*Italians eat Pane al Cioccolato with coffee, or with creamy mascarpone cheese and red wine – a combination which sounds unusual, but which is surprisingly good. These loaves freeze successfully so it is well worth making a batch of four.*

### MAKES 4 LOAVES, EACH WEIGHING ABOUT ¾ lb

| |
|---|
| 1 oz compressed yeast |
| 2½ cups water, at blood heat |
| 6½ cups bread flour |
| ⅓ cup cocoa powder |
| ½ tsp salt |
| 1 tbsp butter |
| 3 tbsp sugar |
| ¼ cup olive oil |
| scant 1 cup semisweet chocolate chips |

Cream the yeast in a warmed bowl with 2 tbsp of the water, then work in 2 tbsp of the flour to make a batter. Cover with oiled plastic wrap and leave in a warm place until spongy – about 30 minutes.

Meanwhile, sift the remaining flour, the cocoa powder and salt into the warmed bowl of a heavy duty (countertop) electric mixer. Work in the butter and sugar. Make a well in the center, add the remaining water, the yeast mixture and olive oil and work with the dough hook until the dough is smooth and elastic. Turn out on to a well floured surface and form into a ball. Clean and grease the bowl, then return the dough to it. Cover the bowl with a sheet of oiled plastic wrap and leave in a warm place until the dough has doubled in bulk, about 1–2 hours.

Turn the dough out on to a floured surface, punch down, then work in the chocolate chips. Cut the dough into 4 equal pieces, form into round loaf shapes and place them well apart on greased baking sheets (2 loaves to a sheet). Cover with oiled plastic wrap and leave to rise again in a warm place until doubled in size – about 30 minutes. Meanwhile, preheat the oven to 425°F.

Uncover the loaves and bake for 10 minutes, then switch the baking sheets around and bake for a further 5 minutes. Reduce the temperature to 375°F and bake for a further 15–20 minutes. Cover the loaves with parchment paper or foil to prevent overbrowning if necessary. Transfer to a wire rack and leave to cool before serving.

# Fruit and Pine Nut Buns

## MARITOZZI

*These deliciously sweet and nutty buns come from Rome, where they were traditionally eaten during Lent, but are now eaten all year round. They are good for breakfast, split and spread with butter – although the Romans prefer to eat them plain.*

**MAKES 12**

| | |
|---|---|
| 2½ cups bread flour | *Topping* |
| 1 oz compressed yeast | 1 egg |
| 6 tbsp water, at blood heat | 1 tsp sugar |
| ⅓ cup sugar | 1 tbsp water |
| ¼ tsp salt | 2½ tbsp coarse sugar or |
| 2 eggs | broken-up rock candy |
| 6 tbsp butter, softened | |
| ⅔ cup golden raisins | |
| ½ cup finely chopped candied fruit | |
| 3 tbsp pine nuts | |

Sift the flour into the warmed bowl of a heavy duty (countertop) electric mixer. Cream the yeast in a separate warmed bowl with 2 tbsp of the water, then work in 2 tbsp of the flour to make a batter. Cover with oiled plastic wrap and leave in a warm place until spongy – about 30 minutes.

Add the sugar and salt to the flour and work until well mixed, then make a well in the center. Add the remaining water, the yeast mixture, eggs and butter in pieces and work with the dough hook until the dough is smooth and elastic. Turn out on to a well floured surface and form into a ball. Clean and grease the bowl, then return the dough to it. Cover the bowl with oiled plastic wrap and leave in a warm place until the dough has doubled in bulk, about 1–2 hours.

Turn the dough out on to a floured surface, punch down, then work in the raisins, candied fruit and pine nuts. Cut the dough into 12 equal pieces, form into oval bun shapes and place them well apart on greased baking sheets. Cover with oiled plastic wrap and leave to rise again in a warm place until doubled in size – about 30 minutes. Meanwhile, place a roasting pan filled with hot water on the floor of the oven and preheat the oven to 375°F. Beat the egg, sugar and water together to make an egg wash for the topping.

Uncover the buns and brush with the egg wash. Sprinkle with the coarse sugar or rock candy and bake for 15–20 minutes or until they are golden brown and sound hollow when tapped on the base. Transfer to a wire rack and leave to cool before serving.

# Florentine Squares

## ———————— STIACCIATA ALLA FIORENTINA ————————

*Stiacciata are traditionally eaten for breakfast on Carnival Thursday in Tuscany, and there are many variations according to the town or city where they are made. The word stiacciata literally means "squashed," and refers to the fact that the cake is always made quite shallow – no more than 1 1/2 inches thick. These orange-flavored, moist and munchy squares of sweet yeast cake are a modern adaptation of an ancient Florentine recipe.*

MAKES TWENTY 2½ inch SQUARES

| |
|---|
| 3¾ cups bread flour |
| 1 oz compressed yeast |
| scant 1 cup water, at blood heat |
| ½ cup lard |
| scant ½ cup sugar |
| pinch of salt |
| finely grated zest of 2 oranges |
| 3½ tbsp freshly squeezed orange juice |
| 4 egg yolks |
| ⅓ cup confectioners' sugar, to finish |

Sift the flour into the warmed bowl of a heavy duty (countertop) electric mixer. Cream the yeast in a separate warmed bowl with 2 tbsp of the water, then work in 2 tbsp of the flour to make a batter. Cover with oiled plastic wrap and leave in a warm place until spongy – about 30 minutes.

Meanwhile, work the lard, sugar, salt and orange zest into the flour. Warm the orange juice to blood heat. Make a well in the center of the flour, add the remaining water, the orange juice, yeast mixture and egg yolks and work with the dough hook to make a smooth and elastic batter. (It will be a little sticky at this stage.)

Spoon into a greased 12 × 10 inch baking pan and press out thinly with the palm of your hand to cover the bottom of the pan. Cover with oiled plastic wrap and leave in a warm place until the dough has risen to the top of the pan, about 1–2 hours. Meanwhile, place a roasting pan filled with hot water on the floor of the oven and preheat the oven to 350°F.

Uncover the dough and bake for 30–35 minutes or until golden brown. Immediately sift the confectioners' sugar over the top and leave to cool in the pan. When completely cold, cut into twenty 2½ inch squares.

# $\mathcal{S}$weet Pear Pizza

## FOCACCIA DI PERE

*A focaccia is a rustic yeast bread from northern Italy, similar to the pizza of the south, although generally thicker. It usually has a savory topping like pizza; this sweet version is less common. Crisp underneath and around the edges, but with a soft, doughy center and sweet juicy pear topping, it makes a wonderful dessert. Apples can be used instead of pears, if preferred.*

### SERVES 6

| |
|---|
| 1⅓ cups bread flour |
| ½ oz compressed yeast |
| ¼ cup milk, at blood heat |
| ¼ cup sugar |
| 1 egg, beaten |
| 5 tbsp butter, softened |
| pinch of salt |
| 2¼ lb ripe Bosc pears |
| juice of 2 lemons |
| ¼ cup apricot jam |
| ½ cup sliced almonds, lightly toasted |

Sift the flour into a warmed bowl. Put the yeast in the warmed bowl of a heavy duty (countertop) electric mixer and gradually blend in the milk, then half of the sugar and 3–4 tbsp of the flour. Cover with oiled plastic wrap and leave to rise in a warm place for 30 minutes to 1 hour or until spongy.

Uncover the bowl and add the beaten egg to the risen yeast batter. Work with the dough hook until incorporated, then add the butter in pieces and work again. Gradually incorporate the remaining flour and the salt until a soft, shiny dough is formed. Turn out on to a well floured surface and form into a ball. Clean and grease the bowl, then return the dough to it. Cover the bowl with oiled plastic wrap and leave in a warm place until the dough has doubled in bulk, about 1–2 hours.

Towards the end of the rising time, prepare the pears. Cut each one in half, peel and core, then place on a plate and sprinkle immediately with half of the lemon juice, to prevent discoloration. Preheat the oven to 425°F.

Turn the dough out on to a greased 13 × 9 inch jelly roll pan. Punch down, then press into the pan, making a rim around the edges. Place the pears, cut side down, on top of the dough and press them down slightly. Pour over any lemon juice from the plate, then sprinkle with the remaining sugar. Bake for 10 minutes, then reduce the temperature to 375°F and bake for a further 20–25 minutes or until the edges are brown and crisp and the center is cooked through. Remove from the oven.

Melt the jam with the remaining lemon juice in a small heavy saucepan. Rub through a sieve, then immediately brush over the pears while they are still hot. Sprinkle the almonds over the top. Serve hot.

# Cakes

## Chestnut Cake

—————— TORTA DI CASTAGNE ——————

*This cake is very moist and heady with rum, with a close texture more like a pudding than a cake. Don't worry if the cake cracks on top during baking: it will flatten slightly on cooling and the cream and chestnut topping will cover any imperfections.*
*The cake, without its cream filling and topping, can be made up to 1 week in advance. After cooling, wrap it closely and store it in an airtight tin. Once the cake has been assembled with the cream it should be kept in the refrigerator. Allow it to come to room temperature for at least 30 minutes before serving so that the full flavor of the cake can be savored.*

### SERVES 8–10

| |
|---|
| 1 cup all-purpose flour |
| pinch of salt |
| 2¼ sticks (9 oz) butter, softened |
| scant 1 cup sugar |
| ¾ lb canned sweetened chestnut purée |
| 9 eggs, separated |
| 7 tbsp dark rum |
| 1¼ cups heavy cream |
| 4–6 marrons glacés, to decorate |

Grease an 8½ inch springform cake pan. Line the bottom with a circle of nonstick parchment paper, then grease the paper. Preheat the oven to 350°F.

Sift the flour and salt into a bowl and set aside. In a separate bowl, beat the butter and ¾ cup of the sugar until light and fluffy, then beat in two-thirds of the chestnut purée a little at a time, alternating with the egg yolks. Fold in the flour until evenly incorporated.

In a separate clean bowl, beat the egg whites until stiff, then fold into the cake mixture until evenly incorporated. Turn the mixture into the prepared cake pan, level the surface and bake for 1 hour or until a skewer inserted into the center comes out clean. Remove the cake from the oven and pierce holes in the top with a fine skewer, then pour over 4 tbsp of the rum. Leave the cake in the pan until completely cold.

Remove the cake from the pan and cut into 2 layers. Whip the cream with the remaining chestnut purée, sugar and rum. Place one layer on a plate and spread with some of the cream mixture. Top with the other layer and swirl over the remaining cream mixture. Decorate with the marrons glacés.

# *Apple Cake*

## ──────── TORTA DI MELE ────────

*Sweet and juicy apples make this simple Genoese sponge moist. Any apple may be used, but Golden Delicious are especially suitable because they retain their shape and crisp texture during baking.*

### SERVES 6

| |
|---|
| 1 cup all-purpose flour |
| 1 tsp baking powder |
| pinch of salt |
| 1½ lb apples |
| 1 tbsp lemon juice |
| 4 eggs |
| ⅔ cup sugar |
| finely grated zest of 1 lemon |
| 7 tbsp butter, melted and cooled |
| confectioners' sugar, to finish |

Grease a 9 inch loose-bottomed cake pan. Line the bottom with a circle of nonstick parchment paper, grease the paper, then dust the bottom and sides of the pan with equal parts of sugar and all-purpose flour, shaking out any excess. Preheat the oven to 350°F. Sift the flour, baking powder and salt together 3 times.

Quarter, core and peel the apples, then slice thinly. As you work, drop them into a bowl of cold water acidulated with the lemon juice (to prevent discoloration).

Put the eggs, sugar and lemon zest in a heatproof bowl. Stand the bowl over a pan of gently simmering water and beat with a hand-held electric beater or rotary or balloon whisk until the mixture is very thick and will hold a ribbon trail on itself when the beater is lifted. Remove the bowl from the heat and continue beating occasionally until the mixture is cool.

Fold in half of the flour mixture, then slowly pour the melted butter around the edge of the mixture and stir it in gently until evenly incorporated. Fold in the remaining flour mixture. Drain and fold in the apples.

Turn the mixture into the prepared cake pan and bake for 40 minutes or until a skewer inserted into the center comes out clean. Leave to cool in the pan for 10–15 minutes, then unmold on to a wire rack and leave to cool completely. Sift confectioners' sugar liberally over the top of the cake before serving.

*Illustrated on page 31*

# Rich Fruit Polenta Cake

## ─── AMOR POLENTA ───

*Sometimes also called Dolce Amor, this moist, fruited yeast cake comes from near the border with Switzerland, around Como and Bergamo, where polenta is such a popular food. Cornmeal gives the cake its characteristic golden-yellow color; the Italians sometimes make it with all polenta flour, which produces a heavy close-textured result, but this version uses a mixture of half cornmeal and half white flour, which is lighter.*

### SERVES 10–12

| |
|---|
| 1¾ cups bread flour |
| 1 oz compressed yeast |
| 1 cup + 2 tbsp water, at blood heat |
| 1⅓ cups raisins |
| 2 tbsp brandy |
| 2 cups yellow cornmeal |
| ¼ tsp salt |
| ¾ cup sugar |
| 1⅓ cups chopped semi-dried figs |
| 2 apples, peeled, cored and chopped |
| ⅔ cup freshly squeezed orange or lemon juice |
| (or a mixture of both) |
| 2 tbsp olive oil |
| 4 tbsp butter, melted |
| beaten egg, to glaze |

Grease a 2 inch deep, 10 inch round cake pan. Dust with cornmeal, shaking out excess.

Sift the flour into the warmed bowl of a heavy duty (countertop) electric mixer. Cream the yeast in a separate warmed bowl with 2 tbsp of the water, then work in 2 tbsp of the flour to make a batter. Cover with oiled plastic wrap and leave in a warm place until spongy – about 30 minutes. Meanwhile, soak the raisins in the brandy.

Stir the cornmeal and salt into the flour, then add the sugar, raisins and brandy, figs, apples and orange or lemon juice. Mix well with the dough hook, then add the remaining water, the yeast mixture, olive oil and melted butter and work with the dough hook until the dough is smooth and elastic. Spoon into the prepared pan, cover with oiled plastic wrap and leave in a warm place until the dough has risen to the top of the pan, about 1–2 hours. Toward the end of the rising time, preheat the oven to 375°F.

Uncover the pan, brush the top of the dough with beaten egg and bake for 50 minutes or until a skewer inserted into the center of the cake comes out clean. Leave to cool in the pan for a few minutes, then unmold carefully on to a wire rack and leave until completely cold before serving.

*Apple Cake & Rich Fruit Polenta Cake*

# *Gianduja Chocolate Cake*

## ——— TORTA GIANDUJA ———

*This is one of the most famous of Italian cakes, from Piedmont in the north-west. The name "Gianduja" is often piped on the top in melted chocolate, but this is not essential. Alternatively decorate with white and dark chocolate rose leaves (see page 125 for how to make them). The name of the cake derives from the gianduja chocolate which is traditionally used in the mixture. It is velvety smooth with a unique flavor, and is available from Italian and other specialty food shops, but a good quality semisweet chocolate can be used if you cannot obtain it. Don't worry if the icing becomes too firm to spread on cooling – simply dip a palette knife in hot water before using to swirl the icing on the cake – it will then spread easily.*

**SERVES 12–15**

| |
|---|
| ¾ cup cornstarch |
| ½ cup all-purpose flour |
| ½ cup cocoa powder |
| pinch of salt |
| ⅔ cup shelled hazelnuts (filberts) |
| 7oz gianduja chocolate |
| 1 stick unsalted butter |
| 6 eggs |
| 3 egg yolks |
| 1 heaping cup sugar |
| ½ cup heavy cream |
| ½ cup Maraschino liqueur or cherry brandy |
| ⅓ cup cherry jam |

Grease a 9½–10 inch springform cake pan. Line the bottom with a circle of nonstick parchment paper, grease the paper, then dust the bottom and sides of the pan with equal parts of sugar and all-purpose flour, shaking out any excess. Sift the cornstarch, flour, cocoa powder and salt together 3 times (to aerate the mixture as much as possible). Set aside.

Put the hazelnuts on a baking sheet and place under a preheated broiler for a few minutes, shaking the sheet frequently until the skins are lightly toasted on all sides. Tip the nuts into a clean dish towel and rub them while they are hot to remove the skins. Discard the skins, then crush the nuts finely in a food processor or electric grinder. Set aside.

Put 3 oz of the chocolate in a double boiler with the butter and half of the crushed nuts. Stir until the chocolate and butter have melted, then remove from the heat and leave to cool, stirring occasionally to prevent a skin forming. Preheat the oven to 325°F.

Put the whole eggs, egg yolks and sugar in a heatproof bowl. Stand the bowl over a pan of gently simmering water and beat with a hand-electric beater or rotary or balloon whisk until the mixture is light and fluffy and will hold a ribbon trail on itself when the beater is lifted. Remove the bowl from the heat and continue beating occasionally until the mixture is cool.

Fold the chocolate mixture into the beaten egg mixture until evenly incorporated, then fold in the sifted flour. Turn the mixture immediately into the prepared pan and tap gently once or twice on the work surface to disperse any air bubbles. Bake immediately for 50 minutes or until a skewer inserted into the center comes out clean.

While the cake is baking, make the chocolate icing. Put the remaining chocolate in a small heavy pan with the cream. Bring to a boil, stirring, then simmer until the chocolate has melted and the mixture is thick. Pour into a metal bowl or pan, stand in a bowl of ice water and leave to cool and thicken to a spreading consistency, stirring occasionally to prevent a skin forming.

When the cake is baked, leave to cool in the pan for 10 minutes, then release the sides of the pan and unmold the cake on to a wire rack. Carefully remove the base and peel off the lining paper. Turn the cake the right way up and place a plate underneath the wire rack. Pierce holes in the top of the cake with a fine skewer and slowly pour over the liqueur or brandy. Leave to cool.

Melt the jam in a small heavy pan, then sieve. Cut the cake into 2 layers. Spread half of the jam over one cut surface of the cake, then about 3 tbsp of the chocolate icing over the other cut surface. Put the cake together again and place on a serving plate with the top (crusty) side underneath. Spread the remaining jam over the top and sides of the cake, then swirl the remaining chocolate icing over the top. Coat the sides and top edge with the remaining crushed nuts.

*Illustrated on page 34*

*Gianduja Chocolate Cake*

# $\mathscr{M}$acaroon and Marsala Cake

## ——— TORTA DI AMARETTI E MARSALA ———

*This simple almond-flavored cake rises well in the oven then shrinks as it cools to make a rich cake with a "puddingy" texture. Serve it with after-dinner coffee and Amaretto liqueur.*

### SERVES 6–8

| |
| --- |
| 3½ cups stale white bread crumbs |
| 2⅓ cups finely crushed amaretti di Saronno cookies |
| 1¼ cups heavy cream |
| ⅔ cup Marsala wine |
| 3 eggs, beaten |
| 4 tbsp butter, melted and cooled |
| 2 tbsp apricot jam |

Grease a 5 cup capacity loaf pan and line the bottom with nonstick parchment paper. Preheat the oven to 350°F.

In a bowl, mix the bread crumbs with 2 cups of the amaretti. Scald the cream in a heavy saucepan, then pour on to the bread crumbs and amaretti and stir well to mix. Add the Marsala, then the eggs and melted butter. Beat the mixture vigorously with a wooden spoon until all the ingredients are thoroughly combined.

Turn the mixture into the prepared pan and level the surface. Bake for 1 hour or until a skewer inserted into the center comes out clean. Leave the cake to cool completely in the pan before unmolding and removing the lining paper.

Melt the apricot jam in a small, heavy saucepan, then sieve and brush over the top of the cake. Sprinkle over the remaining crushed amaretti and press down to adhere to the jam.

# Almond Cake with Coffee Cream Filling

## ———— TORTA DI MANDORLE FARCITA ————

### SERVES 6–8

| | |
|---|---|
| 1¾ cups ground almonds | *Filling* |
| 7 tbsp all-purpose flour | 1¼ sticks (5 oz) unsalted butter, |
| pinch of salt | softened |
| 7 eggs, separated | ¼ cup confectioners' sugar, sifted |
| 6 tbsp sugar | 3 tbsp very strong cold black coffee |
| finely grated zest of 1 lemon | 3 tbsp apricot jam |
| 3 tbsp Apricot Glaze (page 124) | |
| ¼ cup sliced almonds, lightly toasted | |

Grease an 8½ inch springform cake pan. Line the bottom with a circle of nonstick parchment paper, grease the paper, then dust the bottom and sides of the pan with equal parts of sugar and all-purpose flour, shaking out any excess. Preheat the oven to 350°F. Sift the almonds, flour and salt together 3 times.

Put the egg yolks, all but 2 tbsp of the sugar and the lemon zest in a bowl and beat well together with an electric beater until light and fluffy.

In a separate bowl, beat the egg whites until standing in stiff peaks, then beat in the reserved 2 tbsp sugar. Fold a few spoonfuls of egg white into the yolk and sugar mixture to slacken it slightly, then fold in about one-third of the almonds and flour. Continue folding in the remainder in this way, alternating the almonds and flour with egg white until all are incorporated. Turn the mixture immediately into the prepared pan and tap gently once or twice on the work surface to disperse any air bubbles.

Bake immediately for 40 minutes or until the cake is risen and light golden and springy to the touch. Leave to cool in the pan for 10 minutes, then release the sides of the pan and unmold the cake on to a wire rack. Leave until completely cold before removing the base of the pan and peeling off the lining paper.

Make the filling: beat the butter and confectioners' sugar together until light and fluffy, then beat in the coffee a little at a time until evenly incorporated.

Cut the cake into 2 layers. Place the bottom layer on a serving plate and spread the apricot jam over it. Spread coffee butter cream over the jam, then place the other cake layer on top. Brush with the apricot glaze and sprinkle with the nuts. Leave to set before serving.

# $\mathscr{P}$uff Pastry Layer Cake

## ——— DIPLOMATICA ———

*$\mathscr{D}$iplomatica is made up of three layers – pan di spagna (sponge cake), pasta sfoglia (puff pastry) and crema pasticciera (pastry cream). The separate layers can be made up to 2 days in advance, then the cake can be quickly assembled at the last moment. Coat the cake liberally with confectioners' sugar just before serving so that your guests will have a surprise when they first bite into a slice of the cake. The delectable combination of crisp sweet pastry, Maraschino-soaked sponge and creamy filling makes for a luscious treat at any time of day.*

### SERVES 6–8

| | |
|---|---|
| *Puff pastry* | 1 Sponge Cake (page 122) |
| scant 1 cup all-purpose flour | 6 tbsp Maraschino liqueur |
| pinch of salt | about ¼ cup confectioners' sugar |
| 1 stick + 1 tbsp butter | |
| about 3 tbsp ice water | |
| *Pastry cream* | |
| 3 egg yolks | |
| 6 tbsp sugar | |
| ½ cup all-purpose flour | |
| 2¼ cups milk | |

Preheat the oven to 425°F.

Make the puff pastry with the flour, salt, butter and water according to the instructions on page 120. Roll out and cut 2 rounds, each one 9½ inches in diameter. Place on a dampened baking sheet and bake for 8 minutes, then turn them over and bake for a further 2 minutes. Transfer the rounds carefully to a wire rack and leave until completely cold.

Make the pastry cream with the egg yolks, sugar, flour and milk according to the instructions on page 123. Cover the surface with plastic wrap (to prevent a skin forming) and leave to cool.

To assemble the Diplomatica, put one pastry round on a serving plate and spread one-third of the pastry cream over it. Cut the sponge cake into 2 layers and place one layer on top of the layer of pastry cream. Sprinkle with 3 tbsp of the Maraschino. Spread another third of the pastry cream over the cake, then place the remaining cake layer on top and sprinkle with the remaining Maraschino. Spread the remaining pastry cream on top and finish with the remaining round of pastry. Sift confectioners' sugar liberally all over the top and sides of the cake to coat it completely.

# Hazelnut Meringue Cake

## —— MERINGA PRALINATA ALLE NOCCIOLE ——

*This is a special occasion dessert cake which literally melts in the mouth – the crisp meringue on the outside gives way to a lusciously soft marshmallow texture inside. Don't worry if the meringue cracks and splits: it is meant to do so. When assembling the cake, press the top layer gently on to the filling and make sure to chill well for at least 3 hours before slicing so that the cake has time to compress. This will make it much easier to slice.*

### SERVES 6–8

| |
|---|
| 4 egg whites |
| 1 cup superfine sugar |
| 1 cup shelled hazelnuts (filberts), toasted, skinned and ground |
| ½ tsp malt vinegar |
| vanilla extract |
| 1¼ cups heavy cream |
| ½ lb (about 1½ cups) strawberries |
| ½ cup shelled hazelnuts (filberts), toasted, skinned and roughly chopped |
| confectioners' sugar, to finish |

Grease two 8 inch cake pans with butter and line the bottoms with nonstick parchment paper. Dust with flour, shaking out the excess. Preheat the oven to 375°F.

Beat the egg whites until stiff. Add the sugar 1 tbsp at a time and continue beating until the meringue is glossy and standing in peaks. Fold in the ground nuts, vinegar and a few drops of vanilla extract to taste.

Spoon the mixture into the prepared pans and swirl the tops level with a palette knife. Bake for 30 minutes, or until the tops of the meringues are crisp. Unmold carefully on to wire racks, peel off the lining paper and leave to cool.

To make the filling, whip the cream with a few drops of vanilla extract until it just holds its shape. Reserve a few whole strawberries for decoration and slice the remainder. Fold into half the whipped cream. Place one meringue cake on a serving plate and spread with the strawberry cream. Sprinkle the chopped nuts evenly over the cream. Top with the remaining meringue cake, press down gently and dust liberally with sifted confectioners' sugar. Chill for at least 3 hours. Decorate with the reserved whole berries. Serve the remaining cream separately.

# Delicious Cake

## ──── TORTA DELIZIA ────

*T*his cake more than lives up to its name: layers of rum-soaked sponge, pastry cream and homemade almond paste come together to make a deliciously gooey confection. This traditional Italian recipe for Torta Delizia has a "basketweave" of almond paste over both the top and sides of the cake; this requires a certain amount of skill with piping so that the finished cake will look just like a basket, completely covered in almond paste. It is not essential to do this intricate decoration, however; if you prefer a more simple finish, just pipe a lattice or criss-cross pattern over the top of the cake to cover it completely, then pipe around the top edge to give it a neat finish. Press ³⁄₄ cup sliced almonds around the sides.

**SERVES 6–8**

| Sponge cake | Pastry cream |
|---|---|
| 3 eggs | 1 egg |
| 6 tbsp sugar | 1 egg yolk |
| ½ cup + 2 tbsp all-purpose flour | ¼ cup sugar |
| pinch of salt | 5 tbsp all-purpose flour |
| 6 tbsp dark rum | 1⅔ cups milk |
| ¼ cup Sugar Syrup (page 125) | Almond paste |
| scant 1 cup apricot jam | 2⅓ cups blanched almonds |
| 1 egg white, lightly beaten | ¾ cup sugar |
| | 1½ cups confectioners' sugar, sifted |
| | 2 eggs |

Preheat the oven to 350°F.

Make the sponge cake with the eggs, sugar, flour and salt according to the instructions on page 122. Bake in a prepared 8 inch springform cake pan for 30–35 minutes; unmold on to a wire rack and peel off the lining paper. Mix together the rum and sugar syrup. Pierce holes in the top of the cake with a fine skewer and slowly pour over the syrup. Leave to cool.

Meanwhile, make the pastry cream with the whole egg, egg yolk, sugar, flour and milk according to the instructions on page 123. Cover the surface with plastic wrap (to prevent a skin forming) and leave to cool.

Make the almond paste with the almonds, sugars and eggs according to the instructions on page 121.

Line a baking sheet with nonstick parchment paper. Gently heat the jam in a heavy saucepan until melted to a spreading consistency. Slice the cake into 3 equal layers. Put the top layer, crusty side downwards, on the paper. Spread with 3 tbsp of the jam, then with half of the pastry cream. Top with another layer of cake and cover with another 3 tbsp of the remaining jam and pastry cream as before. Cover with the final layer of cake, then coat the top and sides of the cake with the remaining jam.

Basketweave the top of the cake. Put the almond paste in a pastry bag fitted with a ¼ inch tube. Pipe a vertical line of almond paste on top of the cake, starting as near to the left hand edge as possible. Starting again at the left hand edge of the cake, pipe ¾ inch horizontal lines of almond paste across the vertical line, at ¾ inch intervals. Pipe another vertical line from the top edge of the cake, just covering the ends of the horizontal lines. Pipe short horizontal lines in the spaces in between to form the basketweave. Continue in this way, always piping the almond paste down and across, until you reach the opposite (right hand) edge of the cake and the entire top of the cake is covered in basketweave.

Basketweave the sides of the cake. Pipe a vertical line of almond paste from the top edge of the cake to the base, then pipe horizontal lines across and fill in the spaces in exactly the same way as on the top of the cake. Repeat all around the cake until the basketweave meets at the point where you started. Leave the cake in a cool place for 4–6 hours so that the almond paste hardens.

Brush the almond paste with the egg white, then put under a preheated broiler for a few seconds, turning the cake around frequently so that it becomes an even golden brown. Leave to cool, then carefully transfer the cake to a serving plate.

*Illustrated on page 11*

# Fresh Fruit and Cream Genoese

## GENOVESE CON PANNA E FRUTTA

*Raspberries and blueberries have dramatic impact when arranged in rows on top of a cake, but any fresh fruit in season may be used. Golden raspberries combined with red raspberries also look good, or you could make an attractive pattern by using a medley of fresh fruits such as sliced apricots or peaches and cherries as here, or black grapes and strawberries, then brushing them with a very light apricot glaze. Chopped nuts can be used to coat the sides of the cake if liked – green pistachios look very pretty with orange or red fruit.*

**SERVES 6–8**

| | |
|---|---|
| 1 Sponge Cake (page 122) | *Pastry cream* |
| 6 tbsp Sugar Syrup (page 125) | 1 egg |
| 6 tbsp Maraschino liqueur | 2 tbsp sugar |
| 2 cups heavy cream | 3½ tbsp all-purpose flour |
| 3 tbsp vanilla sugar | ¾ cup milk |
| 1⅓ cups fresh sliced peaches | |
| 2 cups fresh cherries | |

First make the pastry cream with the egg, sugar, flour and milk according to the instructions on page 123. Cover the surface with plastic wrap (to prevent a skin forming) and leave to cool.

Slice the sponge cake into 2 layers. Put the top layer, crusty side downwards, on a serving plate. Mix the sugar syrup with the liqueur and drizzle half of this mixture evenly over the cake. Whip the cream with 2 tbsp of the vanilla sugar until it will hold its shape. Spread the pastry cream over the cake, then spread one-third of the whipped cream on top. Cover with the other layer of cake and drizzle with the remaining liqueur mixture as before.

Coat the top and sides of the cake with the remaining whipped cream, swirling or piping it if liked. Arrange the fruit attractively in rows on the top of the cake and sprinkle with the remaining vanilla sugar. Serve as soon as possible, or refrigerate until serving time.

# *Lemon Cake*

## —— TORTA DI LIMONE ——

*This simple cake is similar in texture to a Madeira, but lighter and with a fresh, fruity flavor. The liberal sifting of confectioners' sugar over the cake is a favorite topping with the Italians, but you could drizzle lemon glacé icing over the top, too, if you prefer.*

**SERVES 12**

| |
|---|
| scant 1 cup all-purpose flour |
| 1 cup potato flour |
| 2 tsp baking powder |
| 2 sticks + 1 tbsp butter, at room temperature |
| 1¼ cups sugar |
| finely grated zest of 2 lemons |
| 2 eggs |
| 3 egg yolks |
| 2 tbsp Strega liqueur plus 1 tbsp lemon juice, or 3 tbsp lemon juice |
| confectioners' sugar, to finish |

Grease an 8 inch springform cake pan. Line the bottom with a circle of nonstick parchment paper, grease the paper, then dust the bottom and sides of the pan with equal parts of sugar and all-purpose flour, shaking out any excess. Preheat the oven to 375°F.

Sift the flours and baking powder into a bowl. Put the butter, sugar and lemon zest in a separate bowl and beat together until light and fluffy. Beat the whole eggs and egg yolks together, then add to the creamed mixture a little at a time, beating vigorously after each addition. Beat in a little of the flour mixture if the eggs show signs of separating.

Fold in the remaining flour with a large metal spoon, then gently stir in the liqueur and/or lemon juice. Turn the mixture into the prepared cake pan and level the surface. Bake for 1¼ hours or until a skewer inserted into the center comes out clean. Cover with a piece of parchment paper halfway through the baking to prevent overbrowning. Leave to cool in the pan for 10–15 minutes, then unmold onto a wire rack and leave to cool completely.

To serve, place a wire rack over the cake and sift confectioners' sugar lightly on top. Transfer the cake to a serving plate.

# $\mathcal{N}$ougat Cake with Amaretto and Almonds

———— TORRONCINO ————

*This deliciously gooey cake is named after the famous nougat from Cremona called torrone. Look for it in Italian food shops – it is especially popular around Christmastime, but can be found at other times of year. Although expensive it is well worth buying for this special occasion cake. The nougat is quite hard and chewy and so difficult to crush – cut it into small pieces and chop it finely in a food processor if you find it difficult to crush by hand with a knife. The almond decoration on the top and sides of the cake goes well with the flavors of torrone and Amaretto liqueur, although some versions of Torroncino are decorated with grated chocolate.*

**SERVES 8–10**

| Sponge cake | Torrone cream |
|---|---|
| 6 eggs | 1 stick unsalted butter, softened |
| ¾ cup sugar | 1½ cups confectioners' sugar, sifted |
| 1¼ cups all-purpose flour | 3 tbsp Sugar Syrup (page 125) |
| ¼ tsp salt | 5 oz *torrone*, finely crushed |
| Pastry cream | To finish |
| 1 egg | ½ cup Sugar Syrup (page 125) |
| 1 egg yolk | 6 tbsp Amaretto liqueur |
| ¼ cup sugar | ¾ cup sliced almonds, |
| 5 tbsp all-purpose flour | lightly toasted |
| 1⅔ cups milk | |

Preheat the oven to 350°F.

Make the sponge cake with the eggs, sugar, flour and salt according to the instructions on page 122. Bake in a prepared 9½ inch springform cake pan for 45 minutes; unmold on to a wire rack and peel off the lining paper. Leave to cool.

Meanwhile, make the pastry cream with the egg, egg yolk, sugar, flour and milk according to the instructions on page 123. Cover the surface with plastic wrap (to prevent a skin forming) and leave to cool.

Make the *torrone* cream: beat the butter until light and fluffy, then gradually beat in the confectioners' sugar and sugar syrup until smooth. Fold in the crushed *torrone*.

Beat the pastry cream into the *torrone* cream until evenly incorporated. Slice the cake into 3 equal layers. Put the top layer, crusty side downwards, on a serving plate. Mix the sugar syrup and liqueur together, then drizzle one-third evenly over the cake. Spread a few spoonfuls of the *torrone* filling over the cake. Top with another layer of cake, then drizzle with the liqueur mixture and spread with more *torrone* filling as before. Cover with the final layer of cake, then drizzle with the remaining liqueur mixture. Cover the cake with the remaining *torrone* filling. Arrange sliced almonds around the top edge and the sides.

# Refrigerated Cakes

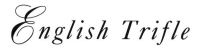

## English Trifle

ZUPPA INGLESE

*T*here must be as many versions of Zuppa Inglese as there are cooks in Italy! Most traditional recipes are very rich, based on ricotta cheese, candied fruit and rum; this lighter version uses fresh strawberries and an orange-flavored liqueur, and is finished with meringue.

SERVES 6–8

| Sponge cake | To finish |
|---|---|
| 3 eggs | scant ½ cup Sugar Syrup |
| 6 tbsp sugar | (page 125) |
| ½ cup + 2 tbsp all-purpose flour | red food coloring |
| pinch of salt | scant ½ cup Aurum liqueur |
| *Pastry cream* | 1½ cups fresh strawberries, |
| 1 egg | hulled and sliced |
| 3 egg yolks | 3 egg whites |
| ½ cup sugar | ⅔ cup superfine sugar |
| ½ cup + 2 tbsp all-purpose flour | |
| 3 cups milk | |

Preheat the oven to 350°F.

Make the sponge cake with the eggs, sugar, flour and salt according to the instructions on page 122. Bake in a prepared deep 6 inch square cake pan for 30–35 minutes, unmold on to a wire rack and peel off the lining paper. Leave to cool. Reduce the oven temperature to 300°F.

Make the pastry cream with the egg, egg yolks, sugar, flour and milk according to the instructions on page 123. Cover the surface with plastic wrap (to prevent a skin forming) and leave to cool.

Cut the sponge cake into ¼ inch thick strips. Put half of the strips in a shallow ovenproof dish. Color the sugar syrup with a few drops of red food coloring and sprinkle over the strips in the dish. Turn the cake over several times until it becomes evenly colored. Put the remaining strips in a separate shallow dish and sprinkle two-thirds of the Aurum over them.

Cover the bottom of a large heatproof glass serving dish with a few spoonfuls of the pastry cream. Place the colored sponge cake on top, then cover with half of the remaining pastry cream. Place the strawberries on top, then the remaining Aurum, cake and pastry cream. Beat the egg whites until stiff, then beat in all but 1 tbsp of the sugar. Pipe on top of the trifle and sprinkle over the remaining sugar. Bake for 20 minutes. Chill before serving.

# $\mathcal{P}$ick Me Up

## —— TIRAMI SU ——

*There are at least two interpretations of the name of this Venetian dessert. One is that the large
amount of liqueur it contains makes it so heady that it has a tonic effect on anyone eating it, and
the other refers to the large number of calories it contains! Rich and creamy with a strong flavor of
coffee and liqueur, Tirami Su is a superb dessert.
Instructions are given here for making this dessert in one large serving bowl, but the mixture can be
divided between 6 individual dessert glasses if preferred, as shown in the photograph.*

### SERVES 6

| |
|---|
| 10 oz mascarpone cheese (about 1¼ cups) |
| 3 tbsp vanilla sugar |
| 2 eggs, separated |
| ¾ cup very strong black coffee |
| scant ½ cup Kahlúa |
| 18 savoiardi (ladyfinger cookies) |
| cocoa powder, to finish |

Put the mascarpone, sugar and egg yolks in a bowl and beat well together. In a separate bowl, beat the egg whites until stiff. Fold the egg whites into the mascarpone mixture until evenly incorporated. Cover the bottom of a serving bowl with a few spoonfuls of the mascarpone mixture.

Mix the coffee and Kahlúa together in a shallow dish. Dip one ladyfinger into the liquid for 10–15 seconds, turning it over so that it becomes well soaked but still retains its shape. Place in the serving bowl. Repeat with 5 more ladyfingers, placing them side by side in the bowl. Cover with one-third of the remaining mascarpone mixture.

Make 2 more layers each of cookies and mascarpone, spreading the top layer of mascarpone smoothly with a palette knife. Sift cocoa powder liberally over the surface, then cover and chill overnight. Serve well chilled.

*Illustrated on pages 50–51*

# *Marsala Cream Mousse*

## —————— BOMBA ALLO ZABAIONE ——————

*This delicately colored dessert is based on the famous Zabaione – a mixture of egg yolks, sugar and Marsala. It is not difficult to make, but it is essential to get the timing right. Follow the method instructions strictly and take care not to be distracted or the gelatin will set before you have had time to beat the egg whites and fold them in.*
*Choose the prettiest-shaped mold you can find for setting the dessert – a fluted one with a hole in the center looks particularly effective. It can be served with a bitter chocolate sauce – simply melt 4 oz bittersweet chocolate with ⅔ cup heavy cream. The bitterness of the sauce contrasts well against the sweetness of the mousse.*

**SERVES 6**

| |
|---|
| 1⅔ cups Marsala wine |
| 4 tsp unflavored gelatin |
| 4 eggs, separated |
| 6 tbsp sugar |
| coffee beans and/or chocolate rose leaves (page 125), to decorate (optional) |

Put 3 tbsp of the Marsala in a cup, sprinkle over the gelatin and leave for about 5 minutes until spongy. Stand the cup in a saucepan of gently simmering water and heat gently until the gelatin has dissolved. Pour ⅞ cup of the remaining Marsala into a measuring cup and stir in the dissolved gelatin. Set aside.

Put the egg yolks in a heatproof bowl with ¼ cup of the sugar. Beat with an electric beater or balloon or rotary whisk until thick and light, then beat in the remaining Marsala a little at a time. Place the bowl over the pan of gently simmering water and continue beating until the mixture is very thick and will hold a ribbon trail on itself when the whisk is lifted.

Remove the bowl from the heat and immediately whisk in the Marsala and gelatin mixture. Stand the bowl in a larger bowl filled with ice water and stir frequently with a spatula until the mixture is cold and beginning to thicken.

Meanwhile, beat the egg whites until stiff, then beat in the remaining sugar until glossy. Fold into the thickened zabaione mousse until evenly incorporated. Pour into a dampened 5 cup capacity fluted mold and level the surface. Cover and chill for 4–6 hours (or overnight) until set.

To serve, carefully ease the mousse away from the side of the mold with your fingertips. Invert a serving plate over the top of the mold and unmold the mousse on to it. Refrigerate until serving time, then decorate with coffee beans and/or chocolate leaves if liked.

*Illustrated on pages 50–51*

*Pick Me Up & Marsala Cream Mousse*

# Punch Cake with Chocolate Ganache Filling

## — PUNSCHTORTE —

*A*s its German name suggests, this multi-layered cake comes from the northern region of Trentino–Alto Adige, near the border with Austria, where the local cuisine is strongly German in character. There are numerous different versions of Punschtorte, some with sponge cake among the layers and some with multi-colored fillings, but one ingredient is common to all – the "punch" or alcohol. As with most punches, rum is the traditional alcohol to use, although you can use brandy or any other spirit or liqueur you prefer.
Both the almond paste and fondant icing can be purchased ready-made, making this a quick and easy cake to prepare. It is deceptively rich and should be cut into very thin slices for serving – ideal for a large buffet party as it makes an exceptionally pretty table centerpiece.

**SERVES 12–15**

| |
|---|
| 8 oz semisweet chocolate, broken into pieces |
| 1 cup heavy cream |
| 5 tbsp unsalted butter |
| 15 oz chocolate-coated graham crackers |
| scant ½ cup dark rum |
| 3 tbsp apricot jam |
| scant ½ quantity (about 7 oz) Almond Paste (page 121) |
| 7 oz fondant icing |
| pink food coloring |
| 1 glacé cherry, to decorate (optional) |

First make the chocolate ganache. Put 7 oz of the chocolate pieces in a heavy saucepan with the cream and butter. Heat gently until melted and smooth, stirring constantly. Pour into a clean cold metal pan or bowl, then place in a bowl filled with ice water. Beat until cold and thick. Remove from the bowl of water, then beat with an electric beater or rotary or balloon whisk until the mixture lightens in color and is very thick and mousse-like.

Roughly crush the graham crackers in a bowl with the end of a straight rolling pin. Add the chocolate ganache and the rum and stir well to mix. Grease a 5 cup capacity mold lightly with oil and line the bottom with nonstick parchment paper. Spoon the mixture into the mold, pressing it down well. Level the surface, cover and chill for about 2 hours or until firm.

Run a palette knife carefully between the bombe and the mold. Invert a serving plate over the mold, then unmold the bombe on to it. Melt the jam in a small heavy saucepan, sieve it and then brush all over the bombe.

Roll out the almond paste thinly on a work surface dusted with confectioners' sugar to a round large enough to cover the bombe. Place over the bombe, press well to adhere, then trim the bottom neatly.

Knead the fondant icing in your hands until pliable, then add a few drops of food coloring and knead again. (Take time over this or the icing will be streaky.) Roll out the icing as for the almond paste. Brush the bombe with hot water, then place the fondant over it, smoothing it gently with the palms of your hands to give the icing a sheen.

Melt the remaining chocolate in a bowl over a pan of gently simmering water (or double boiler), then put into a wax paper pastry bag. Cut a small hole at the tip with kitchen scissors and pipe swirls over the top of the Punchtorte. Decorate the top with a cherry, if liked. Serve at room temperature.

# *Marzipan, Cherry and Ricotta Bombe*

## TORTA ELISABETTA

*Although instructions are given here for making a pale pink bombe topped with white almond paste rosebuds and leaves, with this kind of recipe you can let your imagination run riot as far as color and decoration goes. For a more striking effect, top the bombe with cherries and leaves, using red and green food colorings to color the almond paste before shaping. Any fresh fruit in season can be used in the filling, even candied or glacé fruit in winter. Peaches and apricots go well with the ricotta and almond paste, in which case use Amaretto or Strega liqueur instead of Maraschino.*

**SERVES 8**

| |
|---|
| 1 quantity Sponge Cake batter (page 122) |
| pink food coloring |
| ¾ quantity (about ¾ lb) Almond Paste (page 121), made using egg whites |
| 3 tbsp Maraschino liqueur or cherry brandy |
| finely grated zest and juice of 1 lemon |
| 1 lb 2 oz ricotta cheese (about 2¼ cups) |
| scant ½ cup sugar |
| 1½ cups fresh cherries, halved and pitted |
| confectioners' sugar, to finish (optional) |

Preheat the oven to 350°F. Bake the cake in a prepared deep 10 inch square cake pan for 45–50 minutes; unmold on to a wire rack and peel off the lining paper. Leave to cool.

Dust a 7 cup capacity zuccotto mold or similar bowl or mold with confectioners' sugar and line the bottom with a circle of nonstick parchment paper. Knead a few drops of pink food coloring into two-thirds of the almond paste to color it a delicate pink, then roll out very thinly. Use about three-quarters to line the mold.

Cut the cold sponge cake into strips. Arrange about three-quarters of these strips next to the almond paste, to double line the mold. Mix the liqueur with the lemon juice and sprinkle about three-quarters evenly over the sponge cake, taking care not to make it too wet.

Sieve the ricotta into a bowl, add the sugar and lemon zest and beat well until light and fluffy. Fold in the cherries, then spoon the mixture into the lined mold. Cover with the remaining cake and sprinkle with the remaining liqueur, then cover with the remaining pink almond paste, pressing it down firmly with your hands and tucking in the edge to seal with the sides. Cover the mold with foil, place heavy weights such as cans of food on top and chill overnight.

To serve, remove the weights and foil, then run a palette knife carefully between the bombe and the mold. Invert a serving plate over the mold, unmold the bombe on to the plate and remove the lining paper. Mold the remaining almond paste into rosebuds and leaves. Place on top of the bombe and dust very lightly with sifted confectioners' sugar, if liked.

# Coffee, Chocolate and Cream Pudding

——————— ZUCCOTTO ———————

*The name of this delicious dessert comes from the shape of the mold in which it is traditionally made. Zucca is the Italian word for pumpkin (zuccotto meaning "little pumpkin") and zuccotto molds do indeed look pumpkin-shaped, although in Florence where the dessert originated they say that Zuccotto is shaped just like the cathedral's cupola. Zuccotto molds are not available outside Italy, but a round-bottomed bowl or mold can be used instead.*
*The harlequin effect of the decoration is a little time-consuming, but well worth the effort for a special occasion. Fold a circle of wax paper into 8 sections, then cut out each alternate one. Place over the Zuccotto and sift over the cocoa powder, then move the paper around so that the cocoa powder is covered and sprinkle with the confectioners' sugar. If you are in a rush the Zuccotto can, of course, be simply dusted with either confectioners' sugar or cocoa powder instead of both.*

**SERVES 6**

| | |
|---|---|
| ¾ cup coffee liqueur | *To decorate* |
| 18–20 savoiardi (ladyfinger cookies) | 2 tbsp cocoa powder |
| 1¼ cups heavy cream | 2 tbsp confectioners' sugar |
| ⅓ cup confectioners' sugar, sifted | |
| scant ½ cup shelled hazelnuts (filberts), toasted, skinned and chopped | |
| scant ½ cup shelled almonds, toasted, skinned and chopped | |
| ⅓ cup semisweet chocolate chips | |
| 3 oz semisweet chocolate, broken into pieces | |

Line a 5 cup capacity round-bottomed bowl or mold with damp cheesecloth, leaving it hanging over the rim.

Put all but 3 tbsp of the liqueur in a shallow dish, dip in the ladyfingers one at a time and use to line the bowl or mold, placing them sugared side outwards. Fill the bottom and any gaps with liqueur-soaked trimmings so that the lining is completely solid. Chill for 30 minutes. Reserve the remaining ladyfingers and liqueur.

Whip the cream with the confectioners' sugar until very thick and standing in stiff peaks. Transfer three-quarters to a separate bowl. Stir the nuts and chocolate chips into the remaining one-quarter, then spread this over the ladyfingers to make an inner lining. Return to the refrigerator.

Put the chocolate pieces and remaining 3 tbsp coffee liqueur in a heatproof bowl (or double boiler). Stand the bowl over a pan of gently simmering water and heat gently, stirring occasionally, until the chocolate has melted and is smooth. Remove from the heat and leave to cool slightly, then stir into the remaining whipped cream. Use to fill the center of the bowl or mold and smooth over the surface. Cover with the remaining ladyfingers dipped in the rest of the liqueur. Press the ladyfingers down firmly, then cover with the cheesecloth. Place a plate with heavy weights such as cans of food on top and chill overnight.

To serve, remove the weights and unfold the cheesecloth, then run a palette knife carefully between the cheesecloth and the bowl. Invert a serving plate over the bowl and unmold the Zuccotto on to it. Carefully remove the cheesecloth. Decorate with alternate sections of sifted cocoa powder and confectioners' sugar.

*Illustrated on page 58*

## — MONTE BIANCO —

*M*onte Bianco takes its name from the snow-capped mountain peak Mont Blanc in the French Alps. The dessert originated in Lombardy, although it is now popular in restaurants all over the world. If fresh chestnuts are unavailable, canned whole chestnuts can be substituted, in which case they will not need cooking but can simply be puréed straight from the can. Chestnut purée is also available in cans, but it often contains sugar. For a dessert of this kind it is best to make the purée and sweeten it yourself.

**SERVES 4–6**

| |
|---|
| 1 lb 2 oz chestnuts |
| 2½ cups milk |
| 1 vanilla bean, split |
| ½ cup sugar |
| ¼ cup dark rum |
| 1 cup heavy cream |
| 2 tbsp confectioners' sugar, sifted |

Make a cross in the pointed end of each chestnut with a knife, place in a saucepan of cold water and bring to a boil. Simmer for 15 minutes, then drain. Leave until cool enough to handle, then remove both outer and inner skins with your fingers. Place the skinned chestnuts in a clean saucepan, pour over the milk and add the vanilla bean. Bring to a boil and simmer uncovered for about 45 minutes or until the chestnuts are tender and the milk has been absorbed. Remove the vanilla bean.

Purée the chestnuts in a blender or food processor with the sugar and half of the rum. Leave until cold, then mound into a cone shape in the center of a serving plate.

Whip the cream with the remaining rum and the confectioners' sugar until it will just hold its shape. Spoon over the chestnut "mountain" and serve immediately.

*Coffee, Chocolate & Cream Pudding*

# Chilled Chocolate Cake

## DOLCE FREDDO

*This exceptionally rich sweetmeat is good with after-dinner espresso coffee and liqueurs. It is sometimes served as a dessert with whipped cream, in which case it is best cut into very thin slivers and reserved for those occasions when a light main course precedes it.*

**SERVES 10–12**

| |
|---|
| 7 tbsp unsalted butter, softened |
| 1 cup sugar |
| 2 egg yolks |
| 1 cup + 2½ tbsp cocoa powder |
| ¼ cup Marsala |
| ¾ lb petit beurre or other plain sweet cookies |
| ½ lb amaretti di Saronno cookies |
| confectioners' sugar, to finish |

Grease a 9 × 5 × 3 inch loaf pan and line the bottom with nonstick parchment paper. Put the butter and sugar in a bowl and beat together until light and fluffy (this is best done with an electric mixer). Add the egg yolks, cocoa powder and Marsala and continue beating until all the ingredients are evenly combined.

Put all the cookies in a separate large bowl and crush roughly with the end of a straight rolling pin. Add to the creamed mixture and stir well to mix.

Turn the mixture into the prepared loaf pan and level the surface. Cover and chill overnight.

To serve, run a knife between the cake and the inside of the pan, then invert the cake onto a plate. Peel off the lining paper. Smooth the top and sides of the cake with a palette knife dipped in hot water, then dust lightly with confectioners' sugar.

# Panettone Cake

## PANETTONE FARCITO

*This spectacular-looking cake is very quick and simple to make with a bought Panettone, which can be found in just about every Italian grocery store around Christmastime. If you prefer to make your own Panettone, however, the recipe can be found on page 12.*

**SERVES 8–10**

| |
|---|
| ¾ lb (about 1½ cups) mascarpone cheese |
| 3 eggs, separated |
| ¼ cup sugar |
| ⅔ cup golden raisins |
| ⅓ cup chopped pine nuts |
| ½ cup chopped blanched almonds |
| ½ cup chopped walnuts |
| 1 Panettone |
| ⅔ cup grappa or brandy |
| confectioners' sugar, to finish |

Put the mascarpone in a bowl with the egg yolks, sugar, raisins and nuts. Stir well to combine.

In a separate bowl, beat the egg whites until stiff. Fold into the mascarpone mixture until evenly incorporated.

Cut the Panettone horizontally into 5 slices. Place the bottom slice on a serving plate and sprinkle over 2 tbsp of the grappa or brandy. Spread with one-quarter of the mascarpone mixture. Re-shape the Panettone in this way, sprinkling each layer of cake with 2 tbsp grappa or brandy. Chill until serving time, then sprinkle with confectioners' sugar.

# $\mathscr{C}hocolate\ Salami$

——————— SALAME AL CIOCCOLATO ———————

*Italians from every region seem to have a weakness for this after-dinner sweetmeat that resembles a salami sausage – the trick is to serve it to your guests whole on a board so that it looks as much like a salami as possible. Once sliced the game is given away, but it is fun to deceive everyone, if only for a short while! Take care when serving the salami; it is very rich and should be sliced quite thinly.*

SERVES 12

| |
|---|
| 9 oz amaretti di Saronno cookies |
| 24 graham crackers or other plain cookies |
| 12 oz semisweet chocolate, broken into pieces |
| ¼ cup Amaretto liqueur |
| 2 egg yolks |
| 2¼ sticks (9 oz) unsalted butter, softened |
| ¼ cup ground almonds |

Set aside 2 oz of the amaretti for the decoration. Put the remainder in a bowl with the other cookies and crush roughly with the end of a straight rolling pin. Put the chocolate and liqueur in a large heatproof bowl (or double boiler). Stand the bowl over a pan of gently simmering water and heat gently, stirring occasionally, until the chocolate has melted and is smooth. Remove the bowl from the heat and stir in the egg yolks, then beat in the butter a little at a time until evenly incorporated. Add the crushed cookie mixture and stir well to mix. Leave in a cold place for about 1 hour to firm up the mixture.

Brush a large sheet of wax paper with oil. Turn the mixture on to the paper and shape into a 14 inch long roll with a palette knife. Wrap in the paper, then chill overnight.

To serve, crush the reserved amaretti very finely and mix with the ground almonds. Unwrap the "salami" and roll in the amaretti and almond mixture until evenly coated. Allow to come to room temperature for at least 1 hour before serving.

# Ricotta Pudding

## BUDINO DI RICOTTA

*This rich, creamy pudding is very simple and quick to make. It tastes superb served with fresh red fruit such as strawberries, cherries or raspberries. Sprinkle the fruit with liqueur, or with aceto balsamico, a sharp, balsamic vinegar which can be bought at gourmet food stores. From the ancient city of Modena, balsamic vinegar is believed to have medicinal properties. It is made from very sweet cooked wine mash and is aged for many years in wooden vats. Its delicate perfume and sweet-sour flavor are much loved by the Italians, particularly with sweet fresh fruit.*

### SERVES 6–8

| |
|---|
| 1 lb 2 oz ricotta cheese (about 2¼ cups) |
| ½ cup sugar |
| 4 eggs, separated |
| finely grated zest of 1 lemon |
| ½ cup finely chopped candied fruit |
| ⅔ cup raisins |
| 1¼ cups heavy cream |
| 3 tbsp Strega liqueur |
| ⅔ cup crushed amaretti de Saronno cookies |

Sieve the ricotta into a bowl, add the sugar, egg yolks and lemon zest and beat well together until light and fluffy. Add the candied fruit and raisins and beat well again until evenly mixed.

Whip the cream until it will hold its shape, then fold into the mixture alternately with the liqueur. In a separate clean bowl, beat the egg whites until stiff, then fold into the cheese mixture until evenly incorporated. Pour into individual glasses or a large serving bowl, then chill for 4–6 hours. Sprinkle the crushed amaretti evenly over the top before serving.

# Tarts

## Cherry Custard Tart

—— CROSTATA DI CREMA COTTA ——

*This pretty tart is not unlike the classic French dessert called Clafoutis, except that it is baked in a pastry shell rather than in a dish. In Italy, bottled Maraschino cherries are popular for their strong distinctive flavor of Maraschino liqueur. They are often used in this type of tart in preference to fresh cherries and they certainly make an acceptable alternative.*
*For fresh cherries to retain their plump shape and look good in the custard it is best not to pit them. If you prefer to play safe and pit the cherries, use a mechanical cherry pitter so that the fruit remains whole.*

**SERVES 6**

| | Custard cream |
|---|---|
| 1 quantity Sweet Pie Pastry I (page 118) | 1 egg |
| 1½ cups cherries, stalks removed | 1 egg yolk |
| | 2 tbsp sugar |
| | finely grated zest of ½ lemon |
| | 3½ tbsp all-purpose flour |
| | scant ½ cup milk |
| | ⅔ cup light cream |

Roll out the pastry and line a 9–9½ inch fluted, loose-bottomed tart or quiche mold. Prick the bottom and chill for 30 minutes.

Preheat the oven to 400°F. Line the pastry case with foil and fill with beans.

Bake the pastry case unfilled for 15 minutes; remove the foil and beans and set aside on a wire rack. Reduce the oven temperature to 350°F.

Make the custard cream: put the egg and egg yolk in a bowl, add the sugar and lemon zest and beat together until light and fluffy. Sift in the flour and continue beating until thoroughly incorporated, then add the milk and cream a little at a time, beating well after each addition. Pour the mixture into the pastry case, then stud with the cherries at regular intervals.

Bake for 30 minutes or until the filling is just set in the center. Remove the sides of the mold, transfer the tart to a serving plate and serve as soon as possible, while still warm. Alternatively, transfer the tart to a wire rack and leave to cool before serving.

*Illustrated on pages 66–7*

# Fruit Tartlets with Marsala Cream

## ——— TARTALLETTE ALLA CREMA MARSALA ———

*The filling for these tartlets is a crema pasticciera (pastry cream) made with half Marsala and half milk. The flavor of the Marsala is perfect with the fresh peach or nectarine topping, but you can change the fruit according to what is in season. In wintertime, slices of orange would go well; so too do small seedless grapes.*

*The easiest way to line small molds such as barquettes with pastry is to place a ball of pastry in the center of the mold and press it lightly into shape with your fingertips. As long as the bases are pricked very thoroughly with a fork before baking it is unnecessary to line with foil.*

### MAKES 18

| Sweet pie pastry I | Filling and topping |
|---|---|
| 1⅓ cups all-purpose flour | ⅓ cup sugar |
| ¼ tsp salt | 3 egg yolks |
| ¼ cup sugar | 5 tbsp all-purpose flour |
| 1¼ sticks (5 oz) butter, chilled | ⅔ cup milk |
| 1 egg, beaten | ⅔ cup Marsala wine |
| | 4 medium peaches or nectarines, skinned, pitted and sliced |
| | ⅔ cup hot Apricot Glaze (page 124) |

Make the pastry with the flour, salt, sugar, butter and egg according to the instructions on page 118. Line eighteen 4½ inch long barquette (boat-shaped) molds with the pastry, prick the bases thoroughly and chill for 30 minutes.

Preheat the oven to 375°F. Bake the pastry cases unfilled for 10–15 minutes or until light golden and cooked through. Remove the molds and leave the pastry cases to cool on a wire rack.

Make the filling: put the sugar and egg yolks in a heavy saucepan and stir until evenly blended. Add the flour and beat until smooth, then gradually beat in the milk and Marsala. Place over gentle heat and cook, stirring all the time, until the mixture is very thick. Spoon into the pastry cases and leave to cool.

Arrange the peach or nectarine slices over the filling, then brush with the apricot glaze. Leave to cool and set before serving.

*Illustrated on pages 66–7*

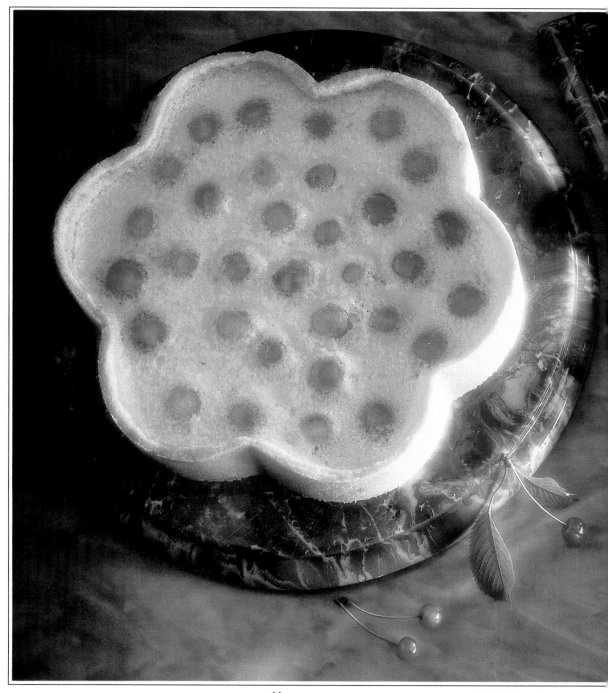

*Cherry Custard Tart*

*Fruit Tartlets with Marsala Cream*

# Pine Nut Tart

## — PINOLATA —

*Pinolata is a sponge cake studded with pine nuts set in a sweet pastry case lined with apricot jam. Pine nuts, called pinoli in Italian, are expensive but quite unique. They are small and elongated in shape, rich and creamy in flavor and texture. They can be found in Italian food shops and gourmet stores. You can, of course, use other, less expensive, nuts in this tart, such as almonds, walnuts or pecans, but the flavor will not be so delicate, and obviously the tart will not be authentic.*

**SERVES 8–10**

| Sweet pie pastry II | Pine nut filling |
|---|---|
| 1⅓ cups all-purpose flour | ⅔ cup sugar |
| ½ tsp baking powder | 1 stick butter, softened |
| pinch of salt | 2 eggs |
| 6 tbsp sugar | 2 egg yolks |
| 1¼ sticks (5 oz) butter | 1½ cups ground almonds |
| 2 medium egg yolks | 3½ tbsp all-purpose flour |
|  | 2 cups pine nuts |
|  | ⅓ cup apricot jam |

Make the pastry with the flour, baking powder, salt, sugar, butter and egg yolks according to the instructions on page 119. Line a 10 inch fluted, loose-bottomed tart or quiche mold with the pastry and prick the bottom. Chill for 30 minutes.

Meanwhile, preheat the oven to 325°F and make the filling. Put the sugar and butter in a bowl and beat together until light and fluffy. Beat in the eggs and egg yolks, then the ground almonds, flour and one-third of the pine nuts.

Spread the apricot jam in the bottom of the pastry case, then spread the pine nut mixture on top and level the surface. Sprinkle with the remaining pine nuts and bake for 40 minutes or until golden. Remove the sides of the mold and leave the tart to cool on a wire rack. Serve at room temperature.

# *Rice Tart*

## ── TORTA DI RISO ──

*Torta di Riso, a delicious pie with an unusual rice pudding filling, is a specialty of Siena. The filling is made with arborio rice, the famous rice from Piedmont used for making risotto, which is cooked with milk, sugar and aromatics until it is soft and sticky, then left to cool overnight.*

### SERVES 6–8

| | |
|---|---|
| 1 quantity Sweet Pie Pastry I (page 118) | *Filling* |
| | 1¾ cups milk |
| 3–4 tbsp hot Apricot Glaze (page 124) | ⅓ cup arborio rice |
| | finely grated zest of 1 lemon |
| | 1 vanilla bean, split |
| | 1 stick unsalted butter, softened |
| | ¼ cup sugar |
| | 2 eggs, separated |
| | 3–4 tbsp apricot jam |

The day before, prepare the rice for the filling. Pour the milk into a heavy saucepan, add the rice, lemon zest and vanilla bean and bring to a boil, stirring. Lower the heat and cook gently, uncovered, for about 45 minutes or until the rice has absorbed the milk and is soft and thick. Take from the heat, remove the vanilla bean, cover the pan and leave the rice to stand in a cold place overnight.

The next day, make the pastry and line a 9–9½ inch fluted, loose-bottomed tart or quiche mold. Prick the bottom and chill for 30 minutes.

Meanwhile, preheat the oven to 350°F and finish making the filling. Put the butter and half of the sugar in a bowl and cream together until light and fluffy. Beat in the egg yolks. Mash the rice with a fork and beat into the creamed mixture a little at a time. In a separate bowl, beat the egg whites until stiff with the remaining sugar. Fold into the rice mixture.

Spread the apricot jam in the bottom of the pastry case, then spread the rice mixture on top and level the surface. Bake for 30–35 minutes or until the pastry is golden and the filling is set and puffed up. Remove from the oven and leave to settle for about 5 minutes, then brush with the apricot glaze. Remove the sides of the mold, transfer the tart to a serving plate and serve warm. Alternatively, transfer the tart to a wire rack and leave to cool before serving.

# $\mathscr{F}resh\ Fruit\ Tart$

## —————— CROSTATA DI FRUTTA FRESCA ——————

*The unusual shape of this tart sets off rows of fresh fruit perfectly, but if you do not have a tranche mold you can equally well use a round mold measuring 9–9½ inches. It will take the same amount of pastry as the tranche used here, but you will have to use double the amount of filling and more fruit, and arrange the fruit in circular rows for a pretty effect. The fruit suggested here is intended only as a guide – you could use any fresh fruit in season. Rows of halved strawberries with slices of kiwi fruit lend themselves beautifully to the tranche shape; so too do tiny wild strawberries on their own, or cherries. Halved grapes can be used in winter. If using pale-colored fruits such as peaches, green grapes and kiwi, then use an apricot jam glaze.*

**SERVES 6–8**

| | |
|---|---|
| 1 quantity Sweet Pie Pastry I (page 118) | *Frangipani filling* |
| | 2 egg yolks |
| about 1 cup raspberries | 3 tbsp sugar |
| about 1 cup red currants, stalks removed | 3½ tbsp all-purpose flour |
| | ⅔ cup milk |
| scant ⅓ cup raspberry jam or currant jelly | ¼ cup ground almonds |
| | 1 tbsp butter, softened |
| 1 tbsp Amaretto liqueur | 1 tbsp Amaretto liqueur |

Roll out the pastry and use to line a 15 × 4½ inch fluted, loose-bottomed tranche mold. Prick the bottom and chill for 30 minutes.

Preheat the oven to 400°F. Line the pastry case with foil and fill with beans. Bake the pastry case unfilled for 15 minutes; remove the foil and beans and bake for a further 7–10 minutes or until golden. Remove the sides of the mold and leave the pastry case to cool on a wire rack.

Make the frangipani filling: put the egg yolks, sugar and flour in a bowl and beat well to mix. Heat the milk to scalding point in a heavy saucepan, then stir into the egg mixture. Return to the rinsed-out pan and heat gently, whisking all the time, until the mixture is thick. Remove from the heat and beat in the almonds, butter and Amaretto. Spoon into the pastry case, spread out evenly with a palette knife, then cover closely and leave to cool.

No more than 1 hour before serving, arrange the raspberries and red currants on top of the filling in rows, alternating the colors. Put the jam or jelly and Amaretto in a heavy saucepan and heat gently until melted, stirring frequently. Boil until thick and syrupy, then sieve and brush all over the fruit. Leave until cold and set before serving. Serve as soon as possible or the juices from the fruit may run into the frangipani filling and glaze and spoil the appearance of the tart.

# *Apple Tart*

## ——— TORTA DI MELE ———

*T*his simple apple tart is made in a pie pan to allow for a decorative edge. Apple shapes complete with stalks and leaves can be cut out from the pastry trimmings and can be painted with pink and green food coloring before baking if liked. Alternatively, you could simply crimp the edge with a fork, make a braided rope or a checkerboard edge, or a deep fluting with your fingers. If you are short of time or prefer something more classically simple, the tart can be baked in a fluted, loose-bottomed tart or quiche mold or a plain flan ring. Do not use baking apples here; most baking apples do not hold their shape well during poaching and baking. Torta di Mele is equally delicious warm or cold, and may be served with cream if wished.

### SERVES 4–6

| Sweet pie pastry I | Filling |
|---|---|
| 1 cup all-purpose flour | 1½ lb apples |
| pinch of salt | 2 tbsp butter |
| 2 tbsp sugar | ¼ cup sugar |
| 1 stick butter, chilled | 1 tsp ground cinnamon |
| 1 egg yolk | Glaze |
| | 1 egg white, lightly beaten |
| | 2 tsp sugar |

Make the pastry with the flour, salt, sugar, butter and egg yolk according to the instructions on page 118. Line an 8 inch pie pan with the pastry, reserving the trimmings for the decoration. Prick the bottom and chill for 30 minutes.

Preheat the oven to 400°F. Line the pastry case with foil and fill with beans. Bake the pastry case unfilled for 10 minutes. Remove the foil and beans and set the case aside on a wire rack. Reduce the oven temperature to 375°F.

To prepare the filling, quarter, core and peel the apples, then slice thinly. Melt the butter in a saucepan, add the sugar and cinnamon and stir to dissolve. Add the apple slices and poach gently for 5 minutes. Turn the apples carefully in the syrup as they cook, taking care that they do not lose their shape. Remove from the heat and tip out on to a cold plate. Leave for a few minutes until cool enough to handle.

Arrange the apple slices in the pastry case, overlapping them in concentric circles. Pour over the poaching syrup. Make decorative shapes from the reserved pastry trimmings and stick them around the edge of the pastry with egg white. Brush with egg white and sprinkle with the sugar for the glaze. Return to the oven and bake for a further 10–15 minutes or until the pastry is golden. Serve warm or cold.

*Illustrated on pages 74–5*

# $\mathscr{A}$pricot Tart

## ———— CROSTATA DI ALBICOCCHE ————

*C*rostata di Albicocche is an all-time favorite with Italians from every region, but it is
particularly popular in the south where apricots grow so prolifically. More often than
not the tart is unadorned – the artistic arrangement of the fruit and the glossiness of the glaze are
attractive enough not to need further embellishment. If you like, you can arrange a few nuts in
between the apricot halves. Almonds or pine nuts would be most appropriate, although green
pistachios provide a prettier color contrast.

### SERVES 8–10

| Sweet pie pastry II | Filling |
|---|---|
| 1⅓ cups all-purpose flour | 2¼ lb fresh apricots |
| ¾ tsp baking powder | ½ cup sugar |
| pinch of salt | 1¼ cups water |
| 6 tbsp sugar | Glaze |
| 1¼ sticks (5 oz) butter | 6 tbsp apricot jam |
| 2 medium egg yolks | ¼ cup Amaretto liqueur |
| 2 tbsp Amaretto liqueur | |

Make the pastry with the flour, baking powder, salt, sugar, butter, egg yolks and Amaretto according to the instructions on page 119. Line a 10 inch fluted, loose-bottomed tart or quiche mold with the pastry, prick the bottom and chill for 30 minutes.

Preheat the oven to 400°F. Line the pastry case with foil and fill with beans. Bake the pastry case unfilled for 15 minutes; remove the foil and beans and bake for a further 8–10 minutes or until golden. Remove the sides of the mold and leave the pastry case to cool on a wire rack.

Halve the apricots and carefully remove the pits. Put the sugar and water in a heavy 10 inch skillet. Heat gently, stirring occasionally, until the sugar has dissolved, then bring to a boil and boil for 3 minutes. Lower the heat and add the apricots, arranging them in a single layer to avoid spoiling their shape. Poach for 5 minutes or until just tender, turning them carefully halfway through this time so that they cook evenly but do not lose their shape.

With a slotted spoon, carefully transfer the apricot halves to a plate lined with paper towels. Leave to drain cut side down for a few minutes, then cut into quarters. Arrange the apricot quarters cut side down in the pastry case. Pour the poaching syrup into a heavy saucepan, add the apricot jam and Amaretto and boil until reduced, thick and syrupy. Sieve, then brush all over the apricots. Leave until cold and set. Serve as soon as possible or the juice from the apricots will run and spoil the appearance of the tart.

*Illustrated on pages 74–5*

*Apple Tart & Apricot Tart*

# Chestnut Tart

## CROSTATA DI MARRONI

*Chestnuts are immensely popular in the northern regions of Italy, in both sweet and savory dishes; chestnut purée is used extensively in desserts and chestnut flour in baking. This tart from Trentino-Alto Adige demonstrates the strong Austrian influence on the cooking of Italy's northernmost region. The almond pastry is similar to the classic Austrian Linzer pastry which is used for the famous raspberry tart called Linzertorte.*
*The method of crumbling the pastry on top of the filling rather than rolling it into a pie lid is unusual and attractive. The dough is rather stiff, but if you can manage to pipe it on to the chestnut purée it will look even more effective.*

**SERVES 4–6**

| Pastry | Chestnut filling |
|---|---|
| 1⅔ cups all-purpose flour | 16 oz can unsweetened chestnut purée |
| ¾ cup ground almonds | |
| 6 tbsp sugar | ½ cup sugar |
| pinch of salt | 2 tbsp water |
| 1¼ sticks (5 oz) butter, softened | pinch of cream of tartar |
| 1 egg | 1 tbsp rum |
| 1 egg yolk | 1–2 tbsp confectioners' sugar, to finish |

Make the pastry: sift the flour, ground almonds, sugar and salt on to a cold work surface. Make a well in the center and add the butter in pieces and then the egg and egg yolk. Work the ingredients lightly together with your fingertips, gradually bringing the flour into the center. Gather the dough into a rough ball, then knead gently on the floured surface until smooth. Wrap and chill for 30 minutes.

Meanwhile, make the filling. Put the chestnut purée in a bowl and mash well with a fork. Put the sugar, water and cream of tartar in a small saucepan and stir over very gentle heat until dissolved. Bring to a boil and boil for 1 minute, then pour into the chestnut purée and beat until well mixed. Add the rum and beat again to mix.

Preheat the oven to 375°F. Cut the pastry in half and use one half to line an 8–9 inch sloping-sided, loose-bottomed tart or quiche mold. Spread the chestnut filling evenly in the pastry case, then crumble the remaining dough evenly over the top. Bake for 30–35 minutes or until the pastry is golden brown. Remove the sides of the mold and leave the tart to cool on a wire rack. Sift confectioners' sugar lightly over the topping just before serving.

# ℛicotta Cheesecake

## ———— CROSTATA DI RICOTTA ————

*T*here are many versions of Crostata di Ricotta from all over Italy, and ingredients vary from one region to another. This version which includes chocolate and candied fruit comes from Sicily where these ingredients are so popular – as in the famous Sicilian refrigerated cake called Cassata Siciliana (page 112).

**SERVES 6–8**

| | |
|---|---|
| 1 quantity Sweet Pie Pastry I | *Ricotta filling* |
| (page 118) | ⅔ cup chopped candied fruit |
| a little egg white, to glaze | ⅔ cup raisins |
| | ¼ cup Marsala wine |
| | 1 lb 2 oz ricotta cheese |
| | (about 2¼ cups) |
| | ¼ cup sugar |
| | 1 egg |
| | 2 egg yolks |
| | finely grated zest of 1 lemon |
| | 2 oz semisweet chocolate, |
| | roughly chopped |

Roll out the pastry and use to line a 9 inch fluted, loose-bottomed tart or quiche mold, reserving the trimmings for the lattice. Prick the bottom and chill for 30 minutes.

Preheat the oven to 400°F. Line the pastry case with foil and fill with beans. Bake the pastry case unfilled for 15 minutes, then remove the foil and beans and set aside on a wire rack. Reduce the oven temperature to 375°F.

Make the filling: put the candied fruit and raisins in a bowl, add the Marsala and stir well to mix. Leave to soak. Sieve the ricotta cheese into another large bowl and beat until light and fluffy. Add the sugar, egg and egg yolks and beat well to mix, then stir in the soaked fruit and liquid, the lemon zest and the chocolate.

Spoon the filling into the pastry case and level the surface. Roll out the remaining pastry and cut 12 strips using a pastry wheel. Arrange in a lattice over the ricotta filling, sticking the ends in place with water. Brush with egg white to glaze and bake for 30–35 minutes or until golden. Remove the sides of the mold and leave the tart to cool on a wire rack before serving. Serve at room temperature.

# *Jam Tart*

—————— CROSTATA DI MARMELLATA ——————

*Crostata di Marmellata is one of the most popular pastries in Italy, and each cook has his or her own way of making it. From simple and inexpensive ingredients, some of the most appealing tarts are made, and Italian pastry shops display what seems like a never-ending stream of different variations of Crostata di Marmellata. The instructions given in the recipe below are for the harlequin tart shown in the photograph. To make a pretty flower tart, fill the pastry case with ⅔ cup apricot jam then cut petal shapes out of the remaining pastry and arrange decoratively on the jam with a glacé cherry as the center of each flower. To make an attractive latticed tart, fill the pastry case with ⅔ cup apricot or plum jam, then cut 8 thin strips out of the remaining pastry, using a pastry wheel to make a crinkled edge. Arrange in a lattice over the jam, sticking the ends in place with water.*

**SERVES 4–6**

| |
|---|
| **1 quantity Sweet Pie Pastry II (page 119)** |
| **⅓ cup plum jam** |
| **⅓ cup apricot jam** |
| **12 yellow glacé cherries** |

Roll out three-quarters of the pastry and use to line a 9–9½ inch fluted, loose-bottomed tart or quiche mold. Prick the bottom. Chill the pastry case and the remaining pastry (well wrapped) for 30 minutes. Meanwhile, preheat the oven to 400°F.

Spoon the jam into the pastry case, alternating the colors for each quarter of the tart. Roll out the remaining pastry and cut 2 thin strips with a pastry wheel. Arrange in a cross over the jam, as illustrated in the photograph, sticking the ends in place with water. Cut out 12 petal or leaf shapes from pastry trimmings and arrange on the uncovered jam. Arrange 3 glacé cherries at the center of each quarter of the tart, as shown in the photograph. Bake for 20 minutes or until the pastry is golden. Remove the sides of the mold and leave the tart to cool on a wire rack before serving.

# Marzipan and Chocolate Pie

## ———— TORTA DI MANDORLE CON CIOCCOLATO ————

*The combination of puff pastry, almond paste and chocolate is obviously very rich, but absolutely divine! Italians use a dark, bitter chocolate for the filling, to contrast with the sweet, sugary almond paste, but it is a matter of personal choice which kind of chocolate you use. Just make sure it is a good quality semisweet or bittersweet chocolate.*

### SERVES 10–12

| Puff pastry | Filling |
|---|---|
| 1¾ cups all-purpose flour | scant 1 quantity (about 14 oz) |
| pinch of salt | Almond Paste (page 121) |
| 2¼ sticks (9 oz) butter | 7 oz semisweet chocolate, |
| ¾–1 cup ice water | broken into small pieces |
| | Glaze |
| | 1 egg |
| | 2 tsp water |
| | 1–2 tbsp sugar |

Make the puff pastry with the flour, salt, butter and water according to the instructions on page 120. Roll out and cut 2 rounds, one 9 inches in diameter, the other 8 inches. Reserve the trimmings.

Preheat the oven to 425°F.

Place the larger round of pastry on a dampened baking sheet. Roll out the almond paste on a work surface sprinkled with confectioners' sugar to an 8 inch round and place on top of the pastry. Scatter the chocolate pieces evenly on top, then place the smaller round of pastry over the chocolate.

Brush the edge of the bottom round of pastry and the outer edge of the top circle with water. Bring the bottom edge up over the top edge, fold it over and press to seal, then flute or crimp. Make leaves or other shapes out of the reserved pastry trimmings and stick them on the top of the pie with water. Beat the egg and water together for the glaze, brush all over the pie and sprinkle with the sugar. Bake for 20 minutes. Transfer carefully to a wire rack and leave to cool. Serve at room temperature.

# $\mathscr{M}$*ixed Nut Tart*

## —— CROSTATA DI NOCI E NOCCIOLE ——

*$H$azelnuts (filberts) and walnuts combine together to make a crunchy topping for this unusual tart. The filling of sponge cake soaked in rum topped with pastry cream provides an excellent contrast in texture.*

### SERVES 8–10

| | |
|---|---|
| ½ quantity Sponge Cake batter (page 122) | *Sweet pie pastry II* |
| | 1¼ cups all-purpose flour |
| 7 tbsp dark rum | ½ tsp baking powder |
| 1 quantity Pastry Cream (page 123) | pinch of salt |
| 1 cup shelled hazelnuts (filberts) | ¼ cup sugar |
| 1¼ cups walnut halves | 1 stick butter, chilled |
| ⅔ cup hot Apricot Glaze (page 124) | 2 egg yolks |
| 2 tbsp sliced almonds | |

Preheat the oven to 350°F.

Bake the sponge cake in a prepared 7 inch springform cake pan for 25 minutes. Unmold on to a wire rack and peel off the lining paper. Leave to cool.

Meanwhile, make the pastry with the flour, baking powder, salt, sugar, butter and egg yolks according to the instructions on page 119. Line a 9–9½ inch sloping-sided, loose-bottomed tart or quiche mold with the pastry. Chill for 30 minutes.

Stir 2 tbsp of the rum into the pastry cream.

Cut the cold sponge cake vertically into thin slices and place in the tart mold, covering the bottom of the pastry case completely. Sprinkle with the rum. Spread the pastry cream evenly on top with a palette knife, then cover with the hazelnuts and walnuts, pressing them down well. Bake for 35 minutes or until the edge of the pastry is golden brown. Leave to settle in the mold for a few minutes, then remove the sides of the mold and leave the tart to cool on a wire rack.

When the tart is completely cold, brush with the hot apricot glaze and arrange the almonds decoratively on top. Leave to cool and set before serving.

# $\mathcal{P}$ear Tart

## CROSTATA DI PERE

*T*he crisp nutty pastry of this crostata contrasts well with the sweet, juicy softness of the pears in the center. Appearance is all-important when it comes to arranging the fan-shaped pears in the pastry case. The best pears to use are Anjou and Comice because of their bulbous shapes.

**SERVES 4–6**

| | |
|---|---|
| 3 ripe pears | *Pastry cream* |
| juice of 1 lemon | 3 egg yolks |
| ¾ cup sugar | 3 tbsp sugar |
| *Pastry* | ⅓ cup all-purpose flour |
| 1¼ cups all-purpose flour | 1¼ cups milk |
| pinch of salt | *Glaze* |
| 6 tbsp butter | 1½ tsp arrowroot |
| ¼ cup finely chopped walnuts | 1 tbsp water |
| 1 tbsp sugar | 1 tbsp apricot jam |
| 1 egg, separated | |
| 2 tbsp very cold water | |

Quarter, core and peel the pears, brushing the exposed flesh with lemon juice to prevent discoloration. Pour 2½ cups water into a heavy saucepan, add the sugar and heat gently until the sugar has dissolved. Add the quartered pears and poach gently for about 20 minutes or until tender.

Meanwhile, make the pastry. Sift the flour and salt into a bowl, cut the butter in pieces, then rub or cut in lightly. Stir in the walnuts and sugar. Beat the egg yolk and water together, make a well in the center of the flour and add the egg mixture. Mix with a knife until the dough draws together, then gather into a rough ball and knead gently on a floured work surface until smooth. Chill for 30 minutes. When the pears are tender, leave to cool in the liquid.

Line an 8 inch tart mold or pie pan with the pastry, using the trimmings to make leaves. Stick the leaves on to the pastry rim with the lightly beaten egg white. Prick the bottom and chill for 15 minutes. Preheat the oven to 375°F. Bake the pastry case unfilled for 15 minutes. Remove from the oven, brush the edge and leaves with egg white and bake for a further 5 minutes.

Make the pastry cream with the egg yolks, sugar, flour and milk as on page 123. Spoon into the pastry case and cover closely. Leave to cool.

Drain the pears and reserve 1¼ cups poaching liquid. Dry the pears with paper towels, then cut each piece into 3 or 4 slices, keeping the stalk end intact. Fan out on top of the pastry cream.

Make the glaze: mix the arrowroot and water in a bowl. Add the jam to the poaching liquid in the pan, heat gently until the jam has melted, then bring to a boil. Stir into the arrowroot mixture, then return to the pan and boil for 2 minutes until thickened. Brush over the pears while hot, then leave to cool and set.

# *Macaroon Tartlets*

─────── TARTELLETTE ALLA CREMA BURROSA ───────

*When baking small tartlet cases unfilled, it is too fiddly to fill each one with baking beans. If you are careful to prick the pastry very thoroughly with a fork and to line the pastry closely and neatly with foil you will find that the beans are unnecessary for small shapes. Piping in the filling gives a neat, professional finish, but you can just as easily spoon in the filling as it levels out during baking and is covered with confectioners' sugar before serving. If you like, put 1 tbsp raspberry jam inside each pastry case before piping or spooning in the macaroon filling.*

**MAKES 8**

| Sweet pie pastry I | Almond cream filling |
|---|---|
| 1⅓ cups all-purpose flour | 5 tbsp butter, softened |
| ¼ tsp salt | 1⅓ cups sugar |
| ¼ cup sugar | 2 eggs, beaten |
| 1¼ sticks (5 oz) butter, chilled | ½ cup ground almonds |
| 1 egg, beaten | 7 tbsp all-purpose flour, sifted |
| | almond extract |
| | confectioners' sugar, to finish |

Make the pastry with the flour, salt, sugar, butter and egg according to the instructions on page 118. Line eight 3–3½ inch fluted, loose-bottomed tartlet molds with the pastry, prick the bases thoroughly and chill for 30 minutes.

Preheat the oven to 375°F. Bake the tartlet cases unfilled (with foil only) for 10 minutes.

Meanwhile, make the filling. Put the butter in a bowl and beat until very soft and creamy. Add the sugar and continue beating, then beat in the eggs, ground almonds, flour and a few drops of almond extract.

Remove the tartlet cases from the oven and discard the foil. Spoon the filling into a pastry bag fitted with a plain vegetable tube and pipe into the pastry cases. Return to the oven and bake for a further 25–30 minutes or until golden. Remove the sides of the molds and leave the pastry cases to cool on a wire rack. Sift confectioners' sugar over the filling before serving.

# $\mathcal{S}$*trawberry Cream Tart*

## —— CROSTATA DI FRAGOLE ——

*$\mathbf{I}$f you can get wild strawberries they look particularly pretty on top of this luscious tart. Whole raspberries look good, too, especially if circular rows of red and golden raspberries are alternated.*

### SERVES 8–10

| Sweet pie pastry I | Filling and topping |
|---|---|
| 1⅓ cups all-purpose flour | 3 egg yolks |
| pinch of salt | 3 tbsp vanilla sugar |
| ⅓ cup sugar | ⅓ cup all-purpose flour |
| finely grated zest of 1 orange | 1¼ cups milk |
| 7 tbsp butter, chilled | 1¼ cups whipping cream |
| 1 medium egg, beaten | 14 oz (about 1 pint) small |
| about 2 tsp freshly squeezed | strawberries |
| orange juice | ⅔ cup hot Strawberry Glaze |
| | (page 124) |

Make the pastry with the flour, salt, sugar, orange zest, butter, egg and orange juice according to the instructions on page 118. Line a 10 inch fluted, loose-bottomed tart pan with the pastry, prick the bottom and chill for 30 minutes.

Preheat the oven to 400°F. Bake the pastry case unfilled for 15 minutes; remove the foil and beans and bake for a further 8–10 minutes or until golden. Remove the sides of the pan and leave the pastry case to cool on a wire rack.

Make the filling: put the egg yolks, vanilla sugar and flour in a bowl and cream together until well mixed. Heat the milk to just below boiling point in a heavy saucepan, then pour slowly onto the creamed mixture, stirring all the time. Return the mixture to the rinsed-out pan and heat gently until thickened, whisking vigorously with a balloon whisk to prevent lumps forming. Remove from the heat, cover the surface closely with dampened wax paper and leave to cool.

Whip the cream until it will hold its shape, then fold into the cooled cream until evenly distributed. Spoon into the pastry case and level the surface.

Cut the strawberries in half lengthwise and arrange in a circular pattern on top of the cream filling. Brush with the strawberry glaze. Leave to cool and set before serving.

# Hazelnut and Chocolate Tart

## —— CROSTATA DI NOCCIOLE CON CIOCCOLATO ——

*For a spectacular finish to this sumptuous tart, make both white and dark chocolate curls to decorate the top. Melt semisweet or sweet chocolate in a bowl over a saucepan of gently simmering water, then pour it on to a very cold, dry surface – marble is ideal. With a palette knife, spread the chocolate thinly backwards and forwards and from side to side until it sets. With a large knife at a 30° angle, push the chocolate away from you, gradually straightening the angle to 90° as the chocolate forms a curl. The sharper the angle, the tighter the curl. Repeat to make more curls, then melt the remaining colored chocolate and proceed as before.*

**SERVES 8–10**

| *Sweet pie pastry II* | *Filling* |
|---|---|
| 1⅓ cups all-purpose flour | ⅔ cup sugar |
| ½ tsp baking powder | 6 tbsp butter, softened |
| pinch of salt | finely grated zest of ½ orange |
| ⅓ cup sugar | 2 eggs, beaten |
| finely grated zest of ½ orange | 1 tbsp all-purpose flour |
| 1¼ sticks (5 oz) butter, chilled | 1¾ cups shelled hazelnuts (filberts), |
| 1 medium egg, beaten | toasted, skinned and ground |
| about 2 tsp orange juice | 3 oz semisweet chocolate, grated |
| | 2 tbsp orange-flavored liqueur |
| | or orange juice |
| | chocolate curls, to decorate |
| | (see introduction above) |

Make the pastry with the flour, baking powder, salt, sugar, orange zest, butter, egg and orange juice according to the instructions on page 119. Line a 10 inch fluted, loose-bottomed tart or quiche mold with the pastry and prick the bottom. Chill for 30 minutes.

Meanwhile, preheat the oven to 400°F and make the filling. Put the sugar, butter and orange zest in a bowl and beat together until light and fluffy. Beat in the eggs and flour, then the ground hazelnuts, chocolate and liqueur or orange juice.

Spoon the filling into the pastry case and level the surface. Bake for 25–30 minutes or until the filling is set. Remove the sides of the mold and leave the tart to cool on a wire rack. Decorate with chocolate curls.

# Cookies & Sweetmeats

## Almond Macaroons

### — AMARETTI —

*Different kinds of amaretti can be found all over Italy, varying in shape, size and texture. This recipe makes small, crisp cookies suitable for serving as petits fours with after-dinner coffee and liqueurs. Almond-flavored Amaretto goes particularly well with them.*
*Bitter almonds are the secret ingredient in amaretti which give the cookies their unique bittersweet flavor, but they are very difficult to obtain outside Italy. Dried apricot kernels, available from health food stores, give a similar bitterness when combined with sweet blanched almonds.*

**MAKES ABOUT 35**

| |
| --- |
| ⅔ cup blanched almonds |
| 2 oz (about ⅔ cup) bitter almonds or apricot kernels |
| ⅔ cup sugar |
| 2 egg whites |
| almond extract |

Preheat the oven to 350°F. Line several baking sheets with nonstick parchment paper.

Grind the nuts (or nuts and apricot kernels) finely in a food processor, then turn into a bowl. Add the sugar, egg whites and a few drops of almond extract and mix well together to a soft, sticky dough.

Fill a pastry bag fitted with a ¼ inch plain tube with the mixture. Pipe 1 inch rounds on the parchment paper, spacing them slightly apart. Bake in batches (2 sheets at a time) for 15 minutes or until browned. Transfer the amaretti on the paper to wire racks and leave to cool.

*Illustrated on page 99*

# $\mathcal{N}$ut Brittle Squares

## —— BISCOTTI CROCCANTI ——

*The nutty topping on these squares is similar to the French Florentines, but instead of being coated on one side with chocolate it is set in a sweet pastry base. The result is very crunchy and quite hard to the teeth – but delicious all the same. Take care when cooking the syrup as it is very hot and bubbles quite fast, especially when the cream and nuts are added. Use thick pot holders when handling the saucepan and the baking sheet with the finished tray of nut brittle on it, to guard against possible splashing.*

**MAKES ABOUT 3 lb**

| Sweet pie pastry I | Topping |
|---|---|
| 1⅓ cups all-purpose flour | 2¾ sticks (11 oz) butter, softened |
| ¼ tsp salt | ⅓ cup clear honey |
| ¼ cup sugar | 1½ cups sugar |
| 1¼ sticks (5 oz) butter, chilled | scant ½ cup heavy cream |
| 1 egg, beaten | 1 cup roughly chopped candied fruit |
| | 1¾ cups sliced almonds |
| | 1½ cups walnut halves |

Make the pastry with the flour, salt, sugar, butter and egg according to the instructions on page 118. Line a 13 × 9 inch jelly roll pan with the pastry and chill while making the filling.

Place a baking sheet (with a lip or rimmed edge) in the oven, and preheat the oven to 400°F.

Put the butter, honey and sugar in a heavy saucepan and cook over moderate heat, stirring frequently, for about 20 minutes or until tawny brown in color. Remove from the heat, leave to settle for 1–2 minutes, then stir in the cream, fruit and nuts. Pour into the pastry case, level the surface and place on the preheated baking sheet. Bake for 20 minutes or until golden brown and bubbling (a little may bubble over the sides on to the sheet). Carefully remove from the oven and leave until completely cold before cutting into squares with a sharp knife.

*Illustrated on page 98*

*Pine Nut Marzipan Bites, Ladies' Kisses & Almond Bites*

*Marguerites & Maraschino Almond Bites*

# Cats' Tongues Cookies

## —— LINGUE DI GATTO ——

*These are the Italian version of the French langues de chats, sometimes also given the more simple name of Biscotti al Burro or "butter cookies." Very thin, crisp and sweet, they make perfect accompaniments for mousses and other creamy desserts. They do not retain their crispness for long, and so must be made within a few hours of serving, but they are very quick and simple.*

**MAKES ABOUT 40**

| |
|---|
| 1 stick butter, softened |
| ⅓ cup sugar |
| ½ egg, beaten |
| ½ egg white |
| scant ¾ cup all-purpose flour, sifted |
| finely grated zest of ½ lemon |
| ½ tsp vanilla extract |

Preheat the oven to 450°F. Line as many baking sheets as you have with nonstick parchment paper.

Put the butter and sugar in a bowl and cream together until light and fluffy. Add the egg and egg white, then the flour, lemon zest and vanilla extract. Mix to a smooth dough.

Fill a pastry bag fitted with a ¼ inch plain tube with the mixture and pipe strips about 3 inches long on the parchment paper, spacing them well apart to allow for spreading. Bake for 3–4 minutes or until browned around the edges. Transfer the cookies on the paper to wire racks and leave to cool. Store in an airtight tin for up to 4 hours before serving.

# *Maraschino Almond Bites*

## —————— MARASCHE ——————

*These deliciously moist sweetmeats are easy to shape as long as you make sure to keep your hands wet while rolling the almond paste around the cherries.*

### MAKES ABOUT 24

| |
|---|
| 1¾ cups ground almonds |
| ¾ cup sugar |
| 2 egg whites |
| almond extract |
| ½ lb jar Maraschino cherries, drained |
| 1 cup sliced almonds, lightly crushed |

Mix together the ground almonds, sugar, all but 2 tsp of the egg white and a few drops of almond extract, working the ingredients to a pliable (not crumbly) almond paste dough.

Preheat the oven to 425°F. Line 2 baking sheets with nonstick parchment paper. Have ready a bowl of cold water.

Dip your hands in the water, then put a walnut-sized piece of almond paste in the palm of one hand. Roll with the palm of the other hand until smooth, then flatten. Put 1 cherry in the center and ease the almond paste around it. Roll in sliced almonds. Repeat with the remaining cherries, almond paste and almonds until all are used up.

Place the Marasche on the parchment paper and bake for 8 minutes. Leave to cool and set for a few minutes, then transfer the Marasche on the paper to wire racks. Leave until completely cold, then place in paper candy (bonbon) cases to serve.

*Illustrated on page 91*

#  Hazelnut Cookies

## — NOCCIOLINE —

**MAKES ABOUT 26**

1 stick butter, softened

¾ cup confectioners' sugar, sifted

¾ cup shelled hazelnuts (filberts), toasted, skinned and coarsely ground

¾ cup all-purpose flour, sifted

½ tsp vanilla extract

about 26 shelled hazelnuts (filberts), to decorate

extra confectioners' sugar, to finish

Preheat the oven to 350°F. Line several baking sheets with nonstick parchment paper.

Put the butter and sugar in a bowl and cream together until light and fluffy. Add the ground hazelnuts, flour and vanilla extract and mix to a fairly firm dough.

With your hands, shape teaspoonfuls of the mixture into rounds. Place them well apart on the parchment paper (to allow for spreading), then press a hazelnut into the center of each. Bake for 12 minutes or until golden brown. Transfer the cookies on the paper to wire racks, dust with confectioners' sugar and leave to cool (they will harden on cooling).

# Marguerites

## MARGHERITE

**MAKES ABOUT 22**

| |
|---|
| 1¼ sticks (5 oz) butter, softened |
| heaping ½ cup confectioners' sugar, sifted |
| 1 egg, beaten |
| 1⅔ cups all-purpose flour |
| vanilla extract |
| about 11 glacé cherries, halved |

Preheat the oven to 475°F. Line 2 baking sheets with nonstick parchment paper.

Put the butter and sugar in a bowl and cream together until light and fluffy. Beat in the egg. Sift in the flour, add a few drops of vanilla extract and beat until evenly incorporated to a soft, smooth dough.

Fill a pastry bag fitted with a ¼ inch star or rosette tube with the mixture. Pipe on to the parchment paper, making whirls 2–2½ inches in diameter. Press half a cherry into the center of each whirl. Bake for 5–6 minutes or until light golden. Transfer the cookies on the paper to wire racks and leave to cool.

*Illustrated on page 91*

# Pine Nut Marzipan Bites

## PINOLATI

**MAKES ABOUT 30**

| |
|---|
| 1¾ cups ground almonds |
| 1½ cups sugar |
| 3 egg whites |
| 2⅓ cups pine nuts |

Mix together the almonds, sugar and 2 of the egg whites, working the ingredients to a pliable (not crumbly) almond paste dough.

Preheat the oven to 450°F.

Put the remaining egg white in a bowl and break up with a fork. Spread the pine nuts out on a plate. Take small pieces of the almond paste in your fingers and roll into about 30 walnut-sized balls. Dip each ball in egg white, then roll in the pine nuts until evenly coated. Put the balls in paper petit four or candy cases and place on baking sheets. Bake for 5 minutes. Transfer to wire racks and leave to cool.

*Illustrated on page 90*

# Polenta Horseshoes

## — KRUMIRI —

*These horseshoe-shaped cookies from Piedmont are made with yellow cornmeal and egg yolks which give them an attractive buttery color. Sometimes the rounded part of the horseshoe is dipped in melted chocolate. For this quantity you will need about 4 oz chocolate.*

**MAKES ABOUT 40**

| |
|---|
| 1 stick butter, softened |
| ¾ cup confectioners' sugar, sifted |
| 2 egg yolks |
| 1 tsp honey |
| finely grated zest of ½ lemon |
| vanilla extract |
| 1¼ cups all-purpose flour |
| ¾ cup yellow cornmeal |

Preheat the oven to 325°F. Line several baking sheets with nonstick parchment paper.

Put the butter and sugar in a bowl and cream together until light and fluffy. Add the egg yolks, honey, lemon zest and a few drops of vanilla extract, then sift in the flour and cornmeal. Mix to a smooth dough.

Break off pieces of the dough and roll into ½ inch thick ropes. Trim and cut into 4 inch lengths. Lift on to the parchment paper and form into horseshoes, spacing them about 2 inches apart. Bake in batches (2 sheets at a time) for 15–20 minutes or until just beginning to brown. Transfer the cookies on the paper to wire racks and leave to cool.

# *Butter Horseshoes*

## —— TORCETTI ——

*Torcetti are often made plain without being dipped in melted chocolate. If you like, you can dip half and leave the other half plain to make an attractive assortment.*

**MAKES ABOUT 36**

| |
|---|
| 6 tbsp butter, softened |
| ⅓ cup sugar |
| 1¾ cups all-purpose flour |
| ¼ tsp baking powder |
| 5 tbsp milk |
| vanilla extract |
| extra sugar, for coating |
| 4 oz semisweet chocolate, broken into small pieces |

Preheat the oven to 400°F. Line several baking sheets with nonstick parchment paper.

Put the butter and sugar in a bowl and cream together until light and fluffy. Sift the flour and baking powder together, then add to the creamed mixture with the milk and a few drops of vanilla extract. Beat until evenly incorporated to a soft, smooth dough, adding a little more milk if necessary.

Break off pieces of the dough and roll into "worm" shapes about 6 inches long and ¼ inch in diameter.

Sprinkle sugar liberally on a board or work surface and roll the pieces of dough in it until quite heavily coated. Form each one into a horseshoe shape and pinch the ends together to seal. Place the Torcetti on the parchment paper and bake in batches (2 baking sheets at a time) for 10–15 minutes or until lightly browned. Transfer the Torcetti on the paper to wire racks and leave to cool.

Put the chocolate pieces in a heatproof bowl (or double boiler). Stand the bowl over a pan of gently simmering water and heat gently, stirring once or twice, until the chocolate has melted and is smooth. Remove the bowl from the pan. Dip the bottom half of each horseshoe in the melted chocolate. Leave to set before serving.

*Illustrated on page 98*

*Butter Horseshoes, Chocolate Kisses & Nut Brittle Squares*

*Almond Macaroons*

# *Chocolate Kisses From Alassio*

## BACI DI ALASSIO

*Crisp on the outside, chewy on the inside, these chocolate cookies will keep quite well in an airtight tin, although the longer they are kept the more chewy they become.*

**MAKES ABOUT 36**

| |
|---|
| 7 oz semisweet chocolate, broken into small pieces |
| 1 cup blanched almonds, toasted and very finely ground |
| 1 cup shelled hazelnuts (filberts), toasted, skinned and very finely ground |
| 1½ cups sugar |
| ⅓ cup cocoa powder |
| 2 tbsp clear honey |
| vanilla extract |
| 3 egg whites |

Preheat the oven to 425°F. Line several baking sheets with nonstick parchment paper.

Put 2 oz of the chocolate pieces in a heatproof bowl (or double boiler). Stand the bowl over a pan of gently simmering water and heat gently, stirring once or twice, until the chocolate has melted and is smooth. Remove the bowl from the pan.

Put the ground nuts in a separate bowl and add the sugar, cocoa powder, melted chocolate, honey and a few drops of vanilla extract. Stir well to mix, then add the egg whites and mix again to form a smooth dough.

Fill a pastry bag fitted with a ¼ inch star or rosette tube with the mixture. Pipe on to the parchment paper, making the star or rosette shapes about 1–1½ inches in diameter. Bake in batches for 8–10 minutes or until set and only just beginning to brown. Transfer the cookies on the paper to wire racks and leave to cool.

Melt the remaining chocolate as before, then use to sandwich the cookies together in pairs. Leave to set before serving.

*Illustrated on page 98*

# *Hazelnut Chewies*

## ——— BRUTTI MA BUONI ———

*The literal translation of brutti ma buoni is "ugly but good," which is an apt description for these cookies. However, they are quite irresistible – crisp on the outside but chewy inside.*

**MAKES ABOUT 20**

| |
|---|
| 1 cup shelled hazelnuts (filberts), toasted, skinned and finely chopped |
| 1 cup confectioners' sugar, sifted |
| 4 egg whites |

Preheat the oven to 400°F. Line 2 baking sheets with nonstick parchment paper.

Put the hazelnuts and confectioners' sugar in a heavy saucepan. Beat the egg whites until stiff in a bowl, then add to the pan. Place the pan over moderate heat and cook for 15 minutes, stirring all the time, until the mixture comes away from the sides of the pan and is a light golden brown.

Remove the pan from the heat. Scoop out the mixture with 2 teaspoons into rough mounds, and place them spaced apart on the parchment paper to allow for slight spreading during cooking. Bake for 10 minutes. Transfer the cookies on the paper to wire racks and leave to cool (they will harden on cooling).

# *Snowballs*

## ——— BOLLE DI NEVE ———

**MAKES ABOUT 25**

| |
|---|
| 1¼ cups shelled hazelnuts (filberts), toasted, skinned and finely ground |
| 3 cups confectioners' sugar, sifted |
| 2 egg whites, lightly beaten with a fork |

Mix together the hazelnuts, 2 cups of the confectioners' sugar and 8 tsp of the egg white, working the ingredients to a firm dough which just binds together.

Preheat the oven to 450°F.

Take heaped teaspoonfuls of the mixture in your hands and roll into about 25 small balls. Dip each in the remaining beaten egg white, then toss in the remaining confectioners' sugar until completely coated.

Lift out on a fork and place in foil petit four or bonbon cases on baking sheets. Bake in the hottest part of the oven for 2 minutes until crisp on the outside but not brown. Cool slightly, then transfer to a wire rack and leave to cool completely.

# *Ladies' Kisses*

## ——— BACI DI DAMA ———

**MAKES ABOUT 40**

| |
|---|
| 1¼ sticks (5 oz) butter, softened |
| ½ cup sugar |
| 1 egg yolk |
| scant ½ cup blanched almonds, toasted and very finely ground |
| ½ cup shelled hazelnuts (filberts), toasted, skinned and very finely ground |
| 1¼ cups all-purpose flour, sifted |
| vanilla extract |
| 2 oz semisweet chocolate, broken into small pieces |

Put the butter and sugar in a bowl and cream together until light and fluffy. Beat in the egg yolk and ground nuts until evenly incorporated, then the flour and a few drops of vanilla extract. Cover the bowl and chill the dough overnight.

The next day, preheat the oven to 325°F. Line several baking sheets with nonstick parchment paper.

Form the dough into rolls about ¾ inch thick, then cut into ½ inch slices. Roll each slice into a small ball in your hands. Repeat to make about 40 balls altogether.

Place the balls on the parchment paper and bake in batches (2 baking sheets at a time) for 20 minutes. Transfer the cookies on the paper to wire racks and leave to cool.

Put the chocolate pieces in a heatproof bowl (or double boiler). Stand the bowl over a pan of gently simmering water and heat gently, stirring once or twice, until the chocolate has melted and is smooth. Remove the bowl from the pan. Use the chocolate to sandwich the cookies together in pairs. Leave to set before serving.

*Illustrated on page 90*

# Hazelnut Crispies

## —— OSSI DEI MORTI ——

*T*he name of these cookies means "dead men's bones" and it is not difficult to see why. Thin and brittle, they even rattle like skeletons when they are shaken in the tin! Ossi dei Morti are traditionally made in Italy for All Souls' Day on November 2. Many different shapes are made according to the region. Sometimes they are fashioned into the shape of ears, noses, legs and arms, other times they are simply shaped into small beans, in which case they are known as Fave dei Morti or "dead men's beans."

### MAKES 30–35

| |
|---|
| 7 tbsp all-purpose flour |
| ¼ tsp baking soda |
| ½ cup sugar |
| ½ cup shelled hazelnuts (filberts), toasted, skinned and finely ground |
| 1 egg white |

Preheat the oven to 375°F. Line several baking sheets with nonstick parchment paper.

Sift the flour and baking soda into a bowl, then stir in the sugar and hazelnuts. Beat the egg white until stiff, then beat into the mixture until evenly incorporated to a soft, sticky dough.

Fill a pastry bag fitted with a ¼ inch plain tube with the mixture. Pipe 2 inch lengths on to the parchment paper, spacing them well apart as the mixture spreads widthwise. Bake in batches (2 baking sheets at a time) for 7–8 minutes or until golden brown. Transfer the cookies on the paper to wire racks and leave to cool (they will harden on cooling).

# *Almond Bites*

## ─── PASTINI DI MANDORLE ───

*These cookies are sweet and crisp, with a short crumbly texture. To serve them as petits fours, the mixture can be baked in paper bonbon cases. Put teaspoonfuls into about 40 cases, make a small hole in the center of each with the handle of the teaspoon, then fill with a little jam. Sprinkle with chopped almonds, then place on baking sheets. Bake them for 12 minutes as they tend to take a little longer this way.*

**MAKES ABOUT 40**

| |
|---|
| 1 stick butter, softened |
| scant 1 cup sugar |
| 1 cup ground almonds |
| 1 egg, beaten |
| almond extract |
| ¾ cup all-purpose flour |
| 1 tsp baking powder |
| about 3 tbsp jam |
| ⅓ cup finely chopped blanched almonds |

Preheat the oven to 400°F. Line several baking sheets with nonstick parchment paper.

Put the butter and sugar in a bowl and beat together until well mixed. Add the ground almonds, egg and a few drops of almond extract, then sift in the flour and baking powder. Mix to a smooth dough.

Put heaped teaspoonfuls of the dough on the parchment paper, spacing them well apart. Put a tiny blob of jam in the center of each and sprinkle with chopped almonds. Bake for 10 minutes. Transfer to wire racks and leave to cool (they will harden on cooling).

*Illustrated on page 90*

# $\mathscr{A}$lmond and Jam Morsels

## BOCCHE DI DAMA

*$\mathcal{S}$weet and dainty, it is not surprising that these cookies are called "ladies' mouthfuls" in Italian. Any kind of jam can be used to sandwich them together, but a combination of half raspberry and half apricot is quite appealing. Sometimes melted chocolate is used rather than jam, but whichever you choose, they will both contrast well with the crisp, short texture of the cookies.*

### MAKES ABOUT 20

| |
|---|
| 1 stick butter, softened |
| 1 cup confectioners' sugar, sifted |
| 1 cup ground almonds |
| ¾ cup all-purpose flour |
| ½ tsp almond extract |
| 8–10 tsp jam |

Preheat the oven to 375°F. Line several baking sheets with nonstick parchment paper.

Put the butter and sugar in a bowl and cream together until light and fluffy. Sift the almonds and flour together, then add to the creamed mixture with the almond extract. Beat until evenly incorporated to a fairly stiff, smooth dough.

Fill a pastry bag fitted with a ¼ inch plain tube with the mixture. Pipe rounds on to the parchment paper, spacing them slightly apart to allow for spreading. Bake in batches (2 baking sheets at a time) for 8–10 minutes or until golden. Transfer the cookies on the paper to wire racks and leave to cool. Sandwich the cookies together in pairs with the jam.

# Regional Specialties

## Easter Tart

―――――――― PASTIERA ――――――――

*Pastiera comes from Naples, where it can be seen in many of the pastry shops at Eastertime. It is an extremely delicious cheesecake – rich, sweet and fruity. Traditionally, Pastiera is made with whole wheat berries, but nowadays canned ready-prepared wheat is used to save time because whole wheat involves long soaking and cooking. Cans of ready-prepared wheat called gran pastiera can be bought at Italian and specialist food stores – you will only need to use half of a 15 oz can for this tart, but the remainder can be frozen and used another time.*

**SERVES 8**

| | |
|---|---|
| 1 quantity Sweet Pie Pastry II (page 119) | scant ½ cup sugar |
| confectioners' sugar, to finish (optional) | 2 eggs |
| | 2 egg yolks |
| *Filling* | ⅓ cup finely chopped candied peel |
| | ½ cup finely chopped walnuts |
| 7 oz canned gran pastiera (see introduction above) | finely grated zest of 1 small orange |
| | finely grated zest of ½ lemon |
| 3½ tbsp milk | ½ tsp orange flower water |
| 1 tbsp butter | ¼ tsp vanilla extract |
| ¾ lb ricotta cheese (about 1½ cups) | pinch of ground cinnamon |

Roll out two-thirds of the pastry and line an 8 inch springform cake pan, pressing it evenly over the bottom and 1½ inches up the sides. Trim the edge neatly and crimp with a fork. Chill with the remaining pastry (well wrapped) for 30 minutes.

Meanwhile, make the filling. Put the gran pastiera in a heavy saucepan with the milk and butter. Cook gently, stirring occasionally, for about 10 minutes until creamy. Turn into a large bowl and cool slightly.

Preheat the oven to 350°F.

Sieve the ricotta cheese into a bowl, add the sugar and beat until light and fluffy. Beat the whole eggs and egg yolks together. Add to the cheese with the gran pastiera and the remaining filling ingredients. Beat well.

Spoon the filling into the pastry case and level the surface. Roll out the remaining pastry and cut into thin strips. Twist the strips and arrange in a lattice over the filling, sticking the ends in place with water. Bake for 1 hour or until the pastry is golden and the filling is set. Leave to cool for 10–15 minutes, then remove the sides of the pan. Transfer the tart to a wire rack. When cold, dust with confectioners' sugar, if liked.

# $\mathcal{F}$ruit and Nut Snail Bread

## ———— GUBANA ————

*T*his delicious pastry which is heavily laden with fruit and nuts gets its name from its shape – guba
is the Slavic word for "snail" – and Gubana comes from Friuli, the region east of Venice, which
is close to the Yugoslav border. It is a traditional Easter bread, the Friulian counterpart to the
Milanese Colomba. This simple version uses puff pastry, but there are other more complicated
versions made with a kind of enriched brioche dough.
Grappa is a coarse, fiery spirit distilled from the stalks, skins and seeds of grapes, like the French
marc. It imparts a bitter taste to Gubana, which contrasts well with the sweetness of the fruits.

### SERVES 12

| *Puff pastry* | *Filling* |
|---|---|
| 1⅓ cups all-purpose flour | 1 cup raisins |
| pinch of salt | scant 1 cup finely chopped walnuts |
| 1¾ sticks (7 oz) butter | ⅔ cup finely chopped candied or |
| 1 tbsp grappa or brandy | glacé fruits |
| about ¼ cup ice water | ⅓ cup pine nuts |
| beaten egg, to glaze | ½ cup fresh bread crumbs |
| confectioners' sugar, to finish | 2 tbsp grappa or brandy |
| | 2 oz semisweet chocolate, |
| | broken into small pieces |
| | 2 tbsp butter |

Make the puff pastry with the flour, salt, butter, grappa or brandy and water according to the instructions on page 120. Roll out on a floured surface to an 18 × 12 inch rectangle and trim the edges square.

Preheat the oven to 425°F. Line a baking sheet with nonstick parchment paper.

Make the filling: mix the raisins, walnuts, candied or glacé fruits, pine nuts and bread crumbs together in a bowl. Sprinkle over the grappa or brandy. Melt the chocolate and butter in a bowl over a pan of gently simmering water, then stir into the filling until evenly mixed.

Spread the filling over the pastry to within 2 inches of the edges. Brush the edges with water, then roll up the pastry from one of the longest sides, keeping the seam underneath as when making a jelly roll. Seal the seam and the ends with water. Transfer to the parchment paper and coil around into a fairly tight snail shape. Brush with beaten egg to glaze, then prick the top with the tines of a fork.

Bake for 15 minutes, then reduce the oven temperature to 325°F and bake for a further 30–35 minutes or until golden brown and crisp. Transfer the Gubana carefully to a wire rack and leave to cool. Serve as soon as possible, sprinkled with confectioners' sugar.

*Illustrated on page 110*

# *Lovers' Knots*

## CENCI

*Cenci are eaten at carnival time in Italy and there are many regional variations. The Italian word cenci means "rags and tatters" which aptly describes these deep-fried scraps of dough. Some regions describe them as Frappe (bows or ties) while the Neapolitans call them Chiacchiere or "chatters," referring to their crisp, light texture. They are made in vast quantities for carnival and eaten throughout the day, especially by the children.*

### MAKES 24

| |
|---|
| scant 1 cup all-purpose flour |
| ½ tsp baking powder |
| pinch of salt |
| 1 tbsp butter |
| 2 tbsp sugar |
| finely grated zest of ½ lemon |
| 1 egg, beaten |
| 1½ tbsp rum or dry white wine |
| vegetable oil, for deep-frying |
| confectioners' sugar, to finish |

Sift the flour, baking powder and salt into a bowl, then rub or cut in the butter with your fingertips. Stir in the sugar and lemon zest. Make a well in the center and add the egg and rum or wine. Mix the ingredients until the mixture comes together as a dough. Turn out on to a well floured surface and knead until smooth. Cover and leave to rest for 20–30 minutes.

Divide the dough into quarters. Roll out each quarter on a well floured surface to a very thin rectangle measuring 6 × 3 inches. Trim the edges to make the corners square, then cut each rectangle into six ½ inch strips. Tie the strips into knots.

Heat the oil in a deep-fryer to 375°F, and deep-fry the Cenci a few at a time until golden and crisp. Remove from the oil with a slotted spoon and drain on paper towels. Dust with sifted confectioners' sugar while still hot. Serve as soon as possible, preferably while slightly warm.

*Illustrated on page 111*

*Fruit & Nut Snail Bread*

# $\mathscr{S}$icilian Chocolate and Ricotta Dessert

## ——— CASSATA SICILIANA ———

$\mathscr{C}$assata Siciliana must be one of the most famous of Italian desserts and yet it is frequently mistaken for Cassata Gelata, an ice cream flavored with pistachio nuts and candied fruits. Cassata Siciliana is not an ice cream but a cake – layers of liqueur-soaked sponge with ricotta cheese and candied fruits. In Sicily it used to be an Easter specialty, but now it is eaten all year round.

**SERVES 6–8**

| | |
|---|---|
| 1 quantity Sponge Cake batter | *Frosting* |
| (page 122) | 7 oz semisweet chocolate, |
| candied fruits, to decorate | broken into small pieces |
| *Filling* | 1½ sticks (6 oz) unsalted butter, cut |
| 1 lb 2 oz ricotta cheese | into small pieces |
| (about 2¼ cups) | scant ½ cup strong black coffee |
| 2 tbsp heavy cream | |
| ¼ cup sugar | |
| 1 tbsp vanilla sugar | |
| ⅓ cup chopped candied fruits | |
| ½ cup Maraschino liqueur | |
| 2 oz semisweet chocolate, grated | |

Preheat the oven to 375°F.

Bake the sponge cake in a prepared 13 × 9 inch jelly roll pan for 15–20 minutes. Unmold on to a wire rack and peel off the lining paper. Leave to cool, then cut widthwise into 3 equal pieces. Brush a 7½ × 3½ × 2½ inch loaf pan very lightly with oil and line the bottom with nonstick parchment paper.

Push the ricotta through a sieve into a bowl, then beat in the cream, sugars, candied fruits and 2 tbsp Maraschino until the mixture is light and fluffy. Add the grated chocolate and beat again until evenly mixed.

Place one piece of cake in the bottom of the prepared pan and sprinkle with 2 tbsp of the Maraschino. Spoon half of the ricotta mixture over the cake and level the surface, then place another piece of cake on top and sprinkle with another 2 tbsp Maraschino. Repeat with the remaining ricotta mixture, cake and Maraschino, then press down. Cover the pan with foil, place heavy weights on top and chill overnight.

The next day, make the frosting. Put the pieces of chocolate and butter in a heatproof bowl (or double boiler), add the coffee and stand the bowl over a pan of gently simmering water. Heat gently, stirring, until the chocolate and butter have melted. Remove from the heat and leave to cool. Chill until thick.

To serve, remove the weights and foil, then run a palette knife carefully between the Cassata and the tin. Invert a serving plate over the pan and unmold the Cassata on to the plate. Remove the lining paper.

Swirl the frosting over the top and sides of the cake, dipping the knife in hot water if necessary. Decorate with candied fruits. Chill until serving time, but allow to come to room temperature before serving.

# *Chocolate, Fruit and Nut Cake*

#### ——— PANFORTE ———

*A Christmas specialty from the town of Siena, Panforte means "strong bread." It is a cross between a cake and confectionery, wonderfully chewy, chocolatey and nuttly with a hint of spiciness. At Christmas, Panforte can be seen in just about every Italian food shop. This homemade version is easy to make and equally as good as any of the packaged commercial varieties. The only tricky part of the method is the sugar boiling – if you have a candy thermometer it is best to use it; it should register 240°F (the soft ball stage). If you overboil the syrup you will find it very difficult to mix evenly into the nut mixture as it tends to stick together in one lump. Finish the mixing with your hands if this is the case and work the mixture to a pliable dough before pressing it into the pan.*

#### MAKES ABOUT 1¼ lb

| |
|---|
| 1 cup shelled hazelnuts (filberts), toasted, skinned and coarsely chopped |
| 1 cup shelled unblanched hazelnuts (filberts), coarsely chopped |
| ½ cup finely chopped candied citron or orange peel |
| 7 tbsp all-purpose flour |
| ⅓ cup cocoa powder |
| pinch each of ground cloves, ground cinnamon and ground white pepper |
| ½ cup sugar |
| ⅓ cup clear honey |
| 2 tbsp unsalted butter |
| a little confectioners' sugar, to finish |

Preheat the oven to 300°F. Line a greased 8 inch springform cake pan with nonstick parchment paper. Mix the nuts and peel together in a bowl. Sift in the flour, cocoa powder and spices and mix well together.

Have ready a glass of ice-cold water. Put the sugar, honey and butter in a heavy saucepan. Heat gently, stirring occasionally, until the sugar has dissolved, then increase the heat and boil for 3–4 minutes or until a little of the mixture forms a soft ball when dropped from a spoon into the glass of water. Immediately pour the syrup into the fruit and nut mixture and stir vigorously to mix together quickly.

Press the mixture into the prepared pan with your fingers, making the top as even and smooth as possible. Bake for 35 minutes. Leave to cool in the pan for 20–30 minutes or until the Panforte hardens slightly (it will be soft when taken from the oven), then remove the sides of the pan and transfer the cake to a wire rack. Remove the base of the pan and the lining paper and leave the cake until completely cold. Dust very lightly with sifted confectioners' sugar and cut into thin wedges to serve.

*Ricotta & Candied Fruit Horns*

*Ricotta Cheese Turnovers*

# $\mathcal{R}$*icotta and Candied Fruit Horns*

## ──────── CANNOLI ────────

*T*ogether with Cassata (page 112), Cannoli are the most famous of all Sicilian desserts. The ricotta cheese and candied fruit mixture is so popular with the Sicilians that they tend to use it in as many different ways as possible. To make authentic Cannoli you will need special metal tube molds which are about 6 inches long and 1 inch in diameter. Unfortunately, these are not readily available outside Italy. The cornet or cornucopia molds used in this recipe are a good alternative; although they are tapered at one end, the general effect is similar.

**MAKES 8**

| Pastry | Filling |
|---|---|
| 1 cup all-purpose flour | 5 oz (about ⅔ cup) ricotta cheese |
| pinch of salt | 2 tbsp vanilla sugar |
| 2 tbsp butter | ½ cup finely chopped candied fruits |
| 1 tsp sugar | 2 tsp orange flower water |
| 3–4 tbsp Marsala or other wine | |
| vegetable oil, for brushing and deep-frying | |
| sifted confectioners' sugar | |

Make the pastry: sift the flour and salt into a bowl, add the butter in pieces and rub in with the fingertips. Stir in the sugar, then just enough wine to bring the mixture together to a fairly firm dough. Form into a ball, wrap and chill for 30 minutes.

Meanwhile, make the filling. Sieve the ricotta cheese into a bowl, add the vanilla sugar and beat until light and fluffy. Add the chopped fruits and the orange flower water and beat again until evenly mixed. Cover and chill while making the Cannoli cases.

Roll out the dough on a lightly floured work surface until very thin – no more than ⅛ inch thick. Cut into eight 4 inch squares.

Brush 8 cornet or cornucopia molds well with vegetable oil. Place a mold diagonally across one pastry square, then roll the pastry up around the mold. Brush the end with water and press to seal. Repeat with the remaining molds and pastry.

Heat the oil in a deep-fryer to 375°F. Deep-fry the Cannoli 1 or 2 at a time for 2–3 minutes or until golden and crisp. Remove from the oil with a slotted spoon and carefully remove the molds if they have not come out in the oil already. Leave the Cannoli cases to drain and cool on paper towels while frying the remainder.

When the Cannoli cases are completely cold, carefully spoon in the filling. Arrange the finished Cannoli on a serving plate and dredge with confectioners' sugar.

*Illustrated on page 114*

# Ricotta Cheese Turnovers

## — CALCIONI —

*Calcioni come from the central region of Marche which borders the Adriatic Sea, but there are many similar "cheesecakes" both large and small, from almost every region in Italy. Some of the Calcioni may pop open during baking, especially if you have not sealed them tightly, but they seem to be just as mouthwatering as the perfectly sealed ones. Calcioni must be eaten warm – the pastry hardens on cooling and they are therefore not so good served cold. If you prefer to eat them cold, substitute puff pastry for the pastry used here and bake the Calcioni at 425°F on a dampened baking sheet. For 10 Calcioni, use a 14 oz package of ready-made frozen puff pastry.*

### MAKES 10

| Pastry | Filling |
|---|---|
| 1⅔ cups all-purpose flour | 6 oz (about ¾ cup) ricotta cheese |
| pinch of salt | ¼ cup sugar |
| 2 eggs, beaten | ½ cup freshly grated Parmesan |
| 2 tbsp olive oil | cheese |
| 1 egg, beaten, to glaze | ⅓ cup golden raisins |
| about 2 tbsp sugar, to dredge | 2 egg yolks |
| | finely grated zest of 1 lemon |
| | 2 tsp lemon juice |

Make the pastry: sift the flour and salt on to a work surface and make a well in the center. Put the eggs and oil in the well and mix together with your fingertips, gradually drawing the flour in from the sides. Add up to 1 tbsp water to bring the mixture together to a smooth, pliable dough. Form into a ball, wrap and chill for 30 minutes.

Meanwhile, make the filling. Sieve the ricotta cheese into a bowl, add the sugar and beat until light and fluffy. Add the remaining filling ingredients and beat again until evenly mixed.

Preheat the oven to 350°F. Line a baking sheet with nonstick parchment paper.

Roll out the dough on a lightly floured surface and cut out 10 rounds with a 4 inch cutter. Brush the edges with water. Place a little filling on one side of each round, then fold the pastry over to half-moon shapes. Press the edges firmly to seal, them crimp with a fork. Place on the baking sheet, brush with beaten egg to glaze and sprinkle with the sugar. Prick the tops with a fine skewer, then bake for 25 minutes until golden. Serve warm.

*Illustrated on page 115*

# Basic Recipes

## Sweet Pie Pastry I

───────────── PASTA FROLLA I ─────────────

*P*asta frolla is rich and sweet, like the classic French pastries pâte sablée and pâte sucrée. The proportion of butter to flour is high, making it quite difficult to work with, but the end result is beautifully crisp and light in texture, melt-in-the-mouth and buttery. As long as you work in cool conditions with cold hands, work surface and utensils, there should be few problems handling the dough. Instructions are given here for rolling or pressing out the dough as soon as it is made. You will find this easier than chilling the dough in a ball directly after making – if the dough is chilled into a ball shape it is difficult to roll, tends to crack and become overworked. Once the dough is rolled or pressed out to its required shape, then is the best time to chill it in the refrigerator – chilling at this stage helps relax the dough and "set" the shape thus preventing shrinkage during baking. This is a crisp pastry suitable for baking unfilled and for use in recipes when a firm, well-shaped pastry case or shell is required. The quantity here gives a generous amount to line a 9–9½ inch tart or quiche mold, allowing extra for decorative trimmings, etc. Individual recipes in this book give different quantities for other sizes and shapes of mold or pan along with different oven temperatures and baking times, but the basic method is the same. Sometimes ice water will be needed to bring the ingredients together as a dough, but the quantity is not specified as flour absorbency varies considerably and egg sizes differ. When mixing the dough with your fingertips, if any water is necessary, add it 1–2 tsp at a time and work it in until the dough holds together without being sticky.

| |
|---|
| 1¼ cups all-purpose flour |
| pinch of salt |
| 3 tbsp sugar |
| 1 stick + 1 tbsp butter, chilled |
| 1 egg yolk |

Sift the flour, salt and sugar on to a cold surface (marble is ideal). Make a well in the center, then add the butter in walnut-sized pieces and the egg yolk. Work the ingredients together with your fingertips or pastry blender, gradually bringing the flour into the center. Work until the ingredients come together as a dough, adding a little ice water if necessary.

Flour the work surface and knead the ball of dough lightly and gently until smooth. The dough is now ready to roll or press out as instructed in individual recipes.

# $\mathscr{S}$weet Pie Pastry II

## —————— PASTA FROLLA II ——————

*T*he method of making this pastry is exactly the same as for Sweet Pie Pastry I. The addition of
baking powder gives a more crumbly result, which is absolutely delicious to eat.
Because of its soft texture, this dough is best used for pies and tarts in which
the filling and pastry are baked together.

| |
|---|
| 1¼ cups all-purpose flour |
| ¼ tsp baking powder |
| pinch of salt |
| ⅓ cup sugar |
| 1 stick + 1 tbsp butter, chilled |
| 1 egg yolk |

Sift the flour, baking powder, salt and sugar on to a cold surface (marble is ideal). Make a well in the center, then add the butter in walnut-sized pieces and the egg yolk. Work the ingredients together with your fingertips or pastry blender, gradually bringing the flour into the center. Work until the ingredients come together as a dough, adding a little ice water if necessary.

Flour the work surface and knead the ball of dough lightly and gently until smooth. The dough is now ready to roll or press out as instructed in individual recipes.

# *P*uff Pastry

## —— PASTA SFOGLIA ——

*M*aking puff pastry at home is not difficult, just time-consuming. The end result – thin layers of buttery crisp, feathery light pastry – is so much better than that of any bought variety, and once you have made the effort you will want to make it again and again. This recipe makes just over a pound of puff pastry, which is more than you will need for most recipes, but as it is so time-consuming, it is worth making more than you need and freezing the remainder. Well wrapped, homemade puff pastry will keep in the freezer for up to 3 months.
Sometimes flavorings such as grappa, brandy and other spirits or liqueurs are used with the water in the dough according to the recipe in which the pastry is to be used. Lemon juice or vinegar can also be added instead of some of the ice water – the acid they contain is said to improve the elasticity of the dough and thus give the pastry more layers.

| |
|---|
| 1⅓ cups all-purpose flour |
| pinch of salt |
| 1¾ sticks (7 oz) butter, chilled |
| about ⅓ cup ice water |

Sift the flour and salt into a bowl. Add about one-quarter of the butter in pieces and rub into the flour with your fingertips, or cut with a pastry blender. Gradually add enough ice water to make the ingredients come together as a fairly stiff dough. Wrap and chill for 30 minutes.

Put the remaining butter on a sheet of nonstick parchment paper, cover with another sheet and pound with a rolling pin into a square shape about ¾ inch thick. After pounding, the butter should be a similar consistency to that of the chilled dough. Unwrap the dough and place on a lightly floured surface. Roll out to a square large enough to envelop the butter. Unwrap the butter and place it diagonally on the dough. Draw up the four corners of the dough around the butter to enclose it as in an envelope. Press the seams together firmly with the rolling pin. Wrap and chill for 15 minutes, to allow the dough to relax.

Unwrap the dough and place on the floured surface again, seam side upwards. Gently roll out to a rectangle three times as long as it is wide, keeping the edges square. Fold the top third down then the bottom third up, so that there are 3 layers of dough. Press the seam and the edges gently with the rolling pin, then turn the dough one-quarter turn to the right and roll out again to a rectangle three times as long as it is wide. Fold the top third down and the bottom third up and seal the edges as before, then wrap and chill for 30 minutes. Repeat this process from first rolling to chilling twice more. After the final chilling the dough is ready to roll out and use as instructed in individual recipes.

# Almond Paste

## —— PASTA DI MANDORLE ——

*H*omemade almond paste, or marzipan, tastes much fresher than any of the bought varieties and it can be mixed in a few minutes in a food processor. In this recipe egg yolks are used to give a good color, but if you prefer a white marzipan, use egg whites instead. Alternatively, 1 whole egg plus 1 yolk or 1 white can be used, according to the exact color required. A few drops of almond extract can be added to heighten the flavor, but if you grind the almonds yourself as here rather than buying ready-ground almonds, you will find the natural almond flavor is quite strong enough. This quantity makes just over a pound of uncooked almond paste.

| |
|---|
| 9 oz (about 2 cups) blanched almonds |
| ½ cup granulated sugar |
| 1 cup confectioners' sugar |
| 2 egg yolks |

Work the blanched almonds in a food processor until they are finely ground. Add the granulated and confectioners' sugar and the egg yolks to the almonds and work again until all the ingredients are evenly mixed. Turn into a bowl and cover with plastic wrap to prevent drying out. Use as soon as possible, within 24 hours.

# $\mathscr{S}$ponge Cake

## —— PAN DI SPAGNA ——

*Literally translated, pan di spagna means "Spanish bread." It came to Sicily from Spain in the early fifteenth century when the Spaniards conquered the island, and the recipe and its name have stood ever since. In fact, pan di spagna is a simple whisked sponge. Light and airy, it is just perfect for the many layered cakes and desserts of which the Italians (and especially the Sicilians) are so fond. It does not keep well, however, and some cooks add melted butter to it, turning it into a Genoese sponge or pasta Genovese, which is also richer and more moist than the plain pan di spagna. This can be done for any of the recipes in this book which call for pan di spagna – simply use 1¼ sticks (5 oz) unsalted butter to each cup of flour, melt and cool it, then fold half of it in with the second batch of flour, the remainder in with the last of the flour.*
*The following 4 egg quantity of cake mixture is sufficient to make a deep 8½ inch cake, which can be cut into 2 or 3 layers. Quantities for different sizes and shapes of pan are given in the individual recipes along with the oven temperatures and baking times, but the basic proportion of ingredients is always the same: 1 egg to 3 tbsp flour and 2 tbsp sugar.*
*Italians add different flavorings according to individual taste: finely grated orange or lemon zest, vanilla or almond extract, or a few drops of a favorite liqueur.*

| |
|---|
| ¾ cup all-purpose flour |
| pinch of salt |
| 4 eggs |
| ½ cup sugar |

Grease an 8½ inch springform cake pan with melted butter. Line the bottom with a circle of nonstick parchment paper, grease the paper, then dust the bottom and sides of the pan with equal parts of sugar and flour, shaking out any excess. Sift the flour and salt 3 times. Set aside.

Preheat the oven to 350°F.

Put the eggs and sugar in a large heatproof bowl. Stand the bowl over a saucepan of gently simmering water, making sure that the bottom of the bowl does not touch the water or the eggs will cook and scramble. Beat with a balloon or rotary whisk or hand-held electric beater until the mixture is thick and light and increased in volume. The mixture should hold a ribbon trail on itself when the beater is lifted. Remove the bowl from the pan and continue beating until cool.

Sift about one-third of the flour over the whisked mixture and fold in lightly and gently with a large metal spoon. Repeat with the remaining flour until it is all incorporated, taking care not to knock out any air.

Pour the mixture into the prepared cake pan, tap gently once on the work surface to disperse any air bubbles, then bake *immediately* for 35 minutes or until the cake is risen and golden. It should feel springy and a warmed skewer inserted in the center should come out clean and dry. Leave to settle for 5 minutes, then transfer to a wire rack. Peel off the paper and leave until cold.

# Pastry Cream

## — CREMA PASTICCIERA —

*T his is the same rich custard made with eggs as the French crème pâtissière. The Italians use it exactly as the French, as a base for fruit in open tarts and as a creamy layer in cakes and gâteaux. The finished cream should be velvety smooth, a texture which is easy to achieve following this basic recipe. If you use a heavy-bottomed saucepan and a wire balloon whisk there should be little risk of curdling or lumps forming, but if you are a little nervous on your first attempt, substitute cornstarch for half of the measured flour – it will help stabilize the mixture. When the cream is finished and off the heat, cover it with plastic wrap while it is still warm, pressing it closely to the surface of the cream to prevent a skin forming.*

*The following basic recipe using 2 egg yolks and 1¼ cups milk makes a fairly thick cream suitable for lining a 7 inch pastry case. Individual recipes in this book may give different proportions of ingredients according to whether a different thickness is required. Some recipes use whole eggs rather than just egg yolks and some use more or less sugar according to the sweetness of other ingredients in the dish in which the cream is used, but the basic method remains the same.*

*Flavorings can be added to the basic cream such as liqueurs, spirits and Marsala wine, the finely grated zest of citrus fruit and vanilla or almond extract. Sometimes the milk is infused with a vanilla bean which gives a gentle aromatic flavor to the finished cream.*

| |
|---|
| **2 egg yolks** |
| **2 tbsp sugar** |
| **3½ tbsp all-purpose flour** |
| **1¼ cups milk** |

Put the egg yolks, sugar and flour in a bowl and cream together until well mixed. Heat the milk to just below boiling point in a heavy saucepan, then pour slowly on to the creamed mixture, stirring all the time. Return the mixture to the rinsed-out pan and heat gently until thickened, whisking vigorously with a balloon whisk to prevent lumps forming.

Remove from the heat and cover the surface of the cream closely during cooling to prevent a skin forming.

# pricot Glaze

## —————— GELATINA D'ALBICOCCA ——————

*P*rofessional pâtissiers and commercial bakers glaze fruit tarts and cakes so that they will retain
their freshness and good looks as long as possible. Sometimes gelatin-based glazes are used and
these often have pectin added to help preserve the natural color of the fruit. At home, glazes are used
to make fruits glisten and shine rather than for their preservative qualities, and this glaze made with
apricot jam does the job simply and extremely well – the addition of lemon juice helps prevent fruit
discoloration. Apricot jam is used for light-colored fruits; strawberry or raspberry jam or currant
jelly is used for red-colored fruits.
For the best effect, always glaze generously. Apply the glaze thickly with a pastry brush in one layer,
working in one direction only. This quantity is sufficient to glaze the top of a 10 inch tart. If you need
less than this, any leftover will keep for several weeks in an airtight container in the refrigerator.
Reheat before use.

| |
|---|
| ½ **cup apricot jam** |
| 2 **tbsp lemon juice** |
| 2 **tbsp brandy or liqueur, according to flavor required** |

Put the jam in a heavy saucepan, add the lemon juice and brandy or liqueur and heat gently, stirring
occasionally, until the jam has melted and is runny. Increase the heat and simmer for 3–5 minutes until thick
and syrupy, then pour through a sieve into a bowl. Use immediately.

# Sugar Syrup

## —————— SCIROPPO DI ZUCCHERO ——————

*Sugar syrup is used in Italian baking for soaking pan di spagna (sponge cake) to make it moist, especially when it is to be layered in a cake. Liqueur is often added to the syrup to give it flavor, and this is always done after the syrup has cooled. Individual recipes in this book specify the type of liqueur appropriate to other ingredients, although Maraschino, Amaretto and Strega are among the most popular. This recipe makes 1¼ cups sugar syrup, which is more than you will need at any one time. It is not worth making in a smaller quantity, however; any leftover will keep indefinitely in an airtight container in the refrigerator.*

| |
|---|
| ½ cup sugar |
| 1¼ cups water |

Put the sugar and water in a heavy saucepan and heat gently, stirring occasionally, until the sugar has dissolved. Increase the heat and boil rapidly for 1 minute, then leave to cool.

# Chocolate Rose Leaves

## —————— FOGLIE DI ROSA DI CIOCCOLATO ——————

*Both white and dark chocolate can be used to make "rose leaves" and the combination of the two colors together looks most effective as a decoration on many cakes, tarts and desserts.*

Wash even-sized unsprayed rose leaves and dry thoroughly with paper towels (if the leaves are wet or greasy the chocolate will not adhere to them properly).

Break chocolate into small pieces and place in a heatproof bowl standing over a pan of gently simmering water. Heat gently until the chocolate melts, stirring only once or twice.

Dip a pastry brush into the melted chocolate, then brush the chocolate evenly onto the underside of the rose leaves, making sure that it does not get onto the top shiny side of the leaves or they will not peel away easily when the chocolate has set.

Place the leaves chocolate-side up on a sheet of nonstick parchment paper and leave in a cool place until set. Peel off the leaves very carefully with your fingers, then chill the chocolate leaves in the refrigerator until ready to use.

# *Index*